Tattletale
A Teacher's Memoir

Carrie Malinowski

PEGASUS BOOKS

Pegasus Books
3338 San Marino Avenue
San Jose, CA 95127
www.pegasusbooks.net

First Edition: March 2015

Published in North America by Pegasus Books. For information, please contact Pegasus Books c/o Caprice De Luca, 3338 San Marino Avenue San Jose, CA 95127.

While the experiences described in *Tattletale* are true as the author knows them to be, her interpretation is entirely her own and completely subjective. Some names and identifying details have been changed to protect the privacy of children who were in her care.

Library of Congress Cataloguing-In-Publication Data
Carrie Malinowski
Tattletale – A Teacher's Memoir/Carrie Malinowski– 1st ed
p. cm.
Library of Congress Control Number: 2015937437
ISBN – 978-1-941859-15-5
1. EDUCATION / Elementary. 2. SELF-HELP / Anxieties & Phobias. 3. SELF-HELP / Personal Growth / Success. 4. BIOGRAPHY & AUTOBIOGRAPHY / Personal Memoirs. 5. HUMOR / Topic / Business & Professional. 6. PSYCHOLOGY / Mental Health. 7. FAMILY & RELATIONSHIPS / Life Stages / School Age.

10 9 8 7 6 5 4 3 2 1

Comments about *Tattletale* and requests for additional copies, book club rates and author speaking appearances may be addressed to Carrie Malinowski at carriemaliowski.com or Pegasus Books c/o Caprice De Luca, 3338 San Marino Ave, San Jose, CA, 95127, or you can send your comments and requests via e-mail to cdeluca@pegasusbooks.net.

Also available as an eBook from Internet retailers and from Pegasus Books

Printed in the United States of America

To
Mrs. Gardener

It was
all worth it!

Stability is the spice of life!

— Carrie Malinowski

AUTHOR'S NOTE

While the experiences I describe in *Tattletale* are true, my interpretation is entirely my own and completely subjective. Some dialogue was burned into my memory by trauma, and some is recreated or quoted from my student teaching journals. To verify my childhood perceptions of teaching, I consulted several veteran teachers who taught during the 1970s and confirmed that it was, indeed, more fun back then.

Teachers are required to keep strict confidentiality. Because of this, I changed the names and some identifying details to protect the privacy of the children who were in my care. Some events have been combined in the interest of clarity. However, teachers Mrs. Hill and Mrs. Gardener, as well as my students, Monica and Tyson, are portrayed exactly as I experienced them.

So get a squirt of sanitizer and come with me. I'll show you around first grade.

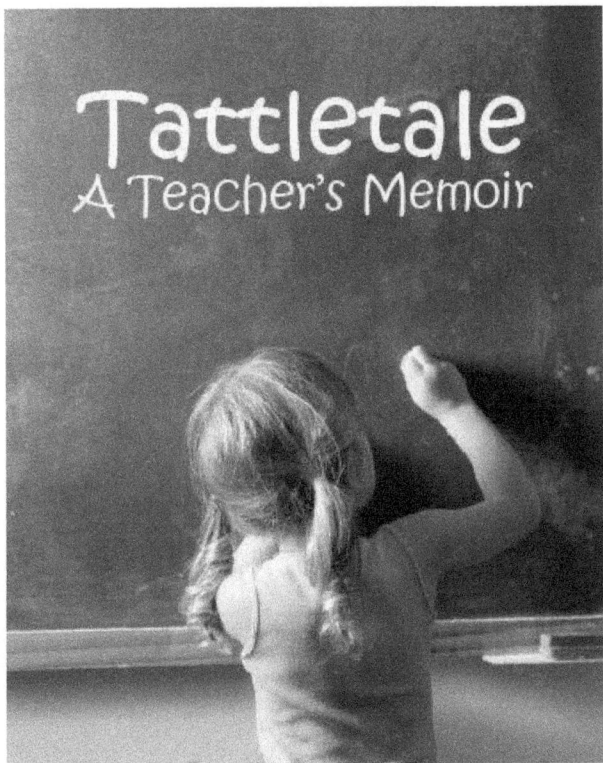

Tattletale
A Teacher's Memoir

The First Year

1
The Naked Screamer

A shriek echoed from the girls' bathroom in back of the class. Out ran a tiny first grader, completely naked and throwing her green plastic scissors.

"I hate school!" little Monica yelled. "I hate *all* of you!"

Pale and skinny, she grabbed what she could from the other students: pencils, crayon boxes, a headband. She flung them across the room.

It was eight-thirty in the morning, and today was the first day of school.

I was the teacher.

2
Eating Yellow Chalk

I'd dreamed of being a teacher since I was four years old. At that age, I had not been to kindergarten yet, but I'd heard about it and played school at home. I knew there was a chalkboard. That seemed to be the most important part, and I had a small one with my own box of chalk.

Yellow chalk was the best for eating because of its smooth feel between my teeth. There had to be kids in school, so I lined up some dolls, a teddy bear, my brother's old GI Joe and the "Ice Bird" from my snow cone maker. Old blue blankie, when arranged in a pile, made a fine student as well.

Where there were students, there must be a teacher. And that was me.

It took a while, over 30 years, to become that teacher. I had, and still have, a sizzling social fear—a tough break for someone whose calling is a career spent in front of people. The constant scrutiny, the sea of eyes.

As an 18-year-old education major, big-hearted and full of hope, I had my first teachers' practicum. In front of my fellow college students, I presented a lesson on how to mix up a batch of pink play dough. The instructor evaluated me as "unsatisfactory." I had failed to make eye contact with my audience.

Failed.

I took this first experience hard—I must have been mistaken about my calling. The shyness grew, cactus-like, into sickness. My stomach churned when I was near people who might judge me. I would never make a good teacher. I sobbed my way through several pillowcases and decided on my second-choice degree: psychology.

I diagnosed myself with social anxiety. Then my disorder and I found a job as a mental health worker at a clinic. I didn't enjoy the job, but I was relieved that there were people much worse off than me.

Jimmy, a client who'd contracted hepatitis, came regularly to my cubicle. The whites of his eyes were a telltale yellow.

"You're just in time," I told him. "I have new teddy bear stickers."

Teaching and its cute supplies were never far from my mind.

"This fuzzy sticker is yours if you get your injection and stop selling sex at the Camp Verde truck stop."

"Why don't you quit working here and just teach little kids?" Jimmy asked. "You'd be really good at that."

He was right. Clinic work was not for me. I couldn't confront ill adults in a mature, direct way. Staying there was worse than looking for something new. I accepted Jimmy's life coaching and got myself a job at a preschool.

My greatest fear in teaching, even in preschool, was having my competence questioned. But I quickly discovered that the worst a preschooler could come up with was, "Your breath stinks."

The kids and I finger-painted and read pretty picture books together. I taught them the letters of the alphabet and how to count. We ate carrots dipped in ranch dressing for snack. I watched over them while they rested on blankets—each with a stuffed dog or bunny under an arm. Before I could say *potty accident*, I'd spent ten years teaching three-year-olds. Ten years! The little girl I'd once been felt at home in that world.

One day the director called me into her office for a meeting. She'd never done this before—not in all those years. A large rock lay in my stomach, possibly covered with slimy, gray moss.

"You aren't going to like this," she said. "*The No Child Left Behind Act* is changing the teaching requirements. You won't qualify for your job anymore with a psychology degree. You need to be certified in Elementary or Early Childhood Education."

The degree I had earned was not enough. Once again, I was unsatisfactory. And now my preschool job would end.

The days hadn't all been blissful, if I was honest with myself, but I didn't want to be forced out either. Now I had to make a choice: go back to casework or go back to college.

We Americans pride ourselves on being descendants of rebels and pioneers. A boisterous spirit is expected, honored. We wouldn't be the land of the free if we were timid and hesitant, and yet *I* was. I was a hard worker, but I had the wrong temperament. No job required someone jittery who was afraid of people, and now even preschool was beyond my reach.

Suddenly, I was done with it. Done with me. I had to make a life for myself, whether I was good enough or not. I decided to face my nightmare, get my teaching certificate, and have the career I'd always wanted.

I made a plan. I'd work at the preschool for as long as I qualified, and spend three nights a week taking classes. Studying and writing papers would be done on the weekends. It would take me three years to complete the certification program.

I'd give up a serious chunk of time with my husband and our little boy, but I was determined to be a teacher—a teacher with students and parents who were fully capable of insulting me, who could stomp the ground and try to make me run.

I could do this job now, I told myself. I could have an elementary school classroom. I was a fully-formed adult. Divorced, remarried. I'd given birth and lost a parent. It was silly now to cower. A little teaching job wasn't bigger than me.

Somewhere inside was that little girl who wanted to write with chalk. She wasn't unsatisfactory. And she'd waited for a real chalkboard long enough.

3
Look What I Did to My Brain

I chose a sparkly new public school for student teaching, a kind of internship in a mentor teacher's classroom. The program supervisor placed me with Mrs. Hill, and I paid several thousand dollars to the college for the privilege of doing her job for a semester, without pay.

Mrs. Hill was in her mid-thirties. Large-butted and sharp-eyed, she had a blonde bob and enviable, milky skin. We'd be teaching first grade together, so before our prep day in her classroom, I bought her a bouquet. I spent some time picking it out. The flowers had to say *friendly*—not *lover*. And I didn't want too much weedy green stuff. White daisies and a yellow ribbon were perfect.

I stood in the doorway of her classroom and held out the bouquet.

"Mrs. Hill? So nice to meet you. I'm your student teacher."

She placed the flowers on the floor, next to a pile of trash.

"Teaching is my passion," she responded.

"Mine, too!" I said. "I'm sure I'll learn a lot from you."

"You will. I spend all my time in my classroom," she went on. "I don't even take 'tinkle' breaks."

I heard later that this lack of basic self-care had landed her in the hospital with a kidney infection, but she prided herself on dedication.

After my years in preschool, I was no stranger to children, reading circles, and parents of all kinds, but I wanted to learn new teaching strategies. I was also struggling to overcome my fear of social situations, the plaguing sizzle under my skin.

Mrs. Hill was a shark, and I arrived in her classroom bleeding drops of anxiety. School started, and she began to eat away at me.

"Don't touch my scissors," she cautioned as I sat down to cut out an art project for her class. The next day, I brought office supplies from home so I wouldn't have to use hers. She snatched the pen out of my hand and demanded, "Did you *steal* this from me?" She guarded her lesson plans like a junkyard dog with fresh rabbit parts.

One afternoon, I taught the first graders a spelling game. Mrs. Hill stood at the back of the classroom and held up a piece of red construction paper with a large "2" printed in black marker. Her lips pursed. As I tried to figure out what she was telling me, she held up another card, "1."

"Keep teaching," she said. "These scores are out of a possible ten and you have a long way to go."

The next morning, my feet dragged as I approached her classroom. *She's in there*, I thought. My mouth went dry.

I paused outside the door and dug around in my purse for something to moisten my lips. I'd bought a tube of grape lip gloss to use while teaching. Now the gloss tasted like *being trapped with Mrs. Hill* and my stomach soured. I wiped it off on the back of my hand. *Go in*, I said to myself. *Go*.

"Good morning, Mrs. Hill. Can I talk to you? I wanted to let you know those rating cards made me uncomfortable yesterday. Could you just give me suggestions instead?"

"You *need* a rating system because you're very confusing to children," she snapped. "It's just the way you are. And no, I can't give you suggestions, because I've already modeled the teaching methods for you. Ask someone *else* your questions from now on!"

I did. The college had assigned me a program supervisor, so I contacted her for help. When I described the problem, she advised, "Personality conflicts are very common in a classroom. Just be professional and work it out."

I stayed with Mrs. Hill for nine weeks, working it out an hour at a time. I watched her badger other staff at the school. She reported their slightest missteps to the principal: the reading specialist violated the dress code by wearing sandals; a substitute let a class be loud in the lunchroom; and an aide went out of turn at the copier.

Mrs. Hill sent school-wide emails, noting the failings of her coworkers and reminding them of school policy. And her comments to me became more critical.

"You might *never* be a teacher."

I could hardly believe she'd say such a thing to my face. My nerves blistered.

One day, her class sat in a circle on the floor while I read a story about frogs and led a discussion on habitats. The kids raised their hands quietly, and I took questions. We looked up the answers in the book. I thought it went well.

"Where do you think you *are*? Owen Charter School?" Mrs. Hill sneered.

After the kids went to recess, I worked up some courage and asked, "What's wrong with Owen Charter?"

"It's a *charter*. The school is trash and the teachers are worse! Those people shouldn't be allowed to work with children."

I excused myself to the ladies room and leaned against the wall to deflect her words in private. It was a struggle to stay in the classroom with Mrs. Hill. With my fear of scrutiny and criticism, I began to have full-blown panic attacks. I'd sweat and vomit and hyperventilate— just putting on a skirt for school.

One morning, Mrs. Hill gave me an assignment: I was to reinforce the concept that sentences start with a capital letter. I walked to the overhead projector near the front of the room and began to write a simple sentence with a dry erase marker.

"Don't touch my overhead projector! And don't wipe that mark off with your finger," she stormed.

The kids went silent. As I stepped back, Jared in the first row stuck his foot out. I lost my balance and fell against the whiteboard. Mrs. Hill didn't reprimand him. Neither did I. I understood the rules: I had no authority, no value, and no place in her classroom.

"These students don't respect you, and they have no reason to," she announced to all of us. "Teaching will be a battle for you from now on." It was a curse. "And don't *think* of using a tissue on my projector, either. I have a special cloth for that purpose and you should *know* that by now. As a teacher, you have a responsibility to be prepared with every item you need for this lesson."

The clean cloth had been there that morning. I wondered if Mrs. Hill had taken it. Or maybe Jared had it in his desk.

"*She's* not a teacher!" Jared said.

"Even a child knows," Mrs. Hill sneered.

I stared into the white light of the projector, a metallic taste creeping up the back of my throat. Little bursts of light popped around the edges of my vision. *What* had I been saying? My upper lip went cold and sweaty. Jared laughed. I stumbled out into the hallway, and everything dissolved into black as I fainted.

I came to, alone, and crawled along the nubby carpet to the nurse's office in a nauseous gray fog. Mrs. Hill had her own way of teaching. I lay on the nurse's scratchy cot—sweaty, ashamed—but relieved to be out of sight and away from Mrs. Hill and Jared. The nurse gave me a tiny carton of orange juice to sip while she placed her cool hand on my forehead. Her kindness felt foreign to me in the world of Mrs. Hill.

The next morning was my mid-term evaluation. Mrs. Hill and my program supervisor were scheduled to observe and evaluate me teaching a formal math lesson. I'd been dreading it anyway, and fainting yesterday didn't help my confidence. However, I arrived fully prepared to demonstrate geometric attributes, using edible "manipulatives" that I had purchased for the kids myself: fruit leather cut into triangles, gingersnaps for circles, and cheese rectangles. I'd rehearsed and lost sleep for several nights. A dull ache pounded behind my left eye.

A few minutes before my presentation, Mrs. Hill walked toward the door of her classroom.

"I'll be right back. You go ahead and start your midterm lesson."

I handed out napkins and the edible shapes, smiling at the kids.

"We'll have our shapes activity in just a minute. Don't eat these yet." Most of them smiled back.

Jared shoved a fruit leather triangle into his mouth.

"This is gonna be dumb," he said.

I ignored Jared and read the kids a story while we waited for Mrs. Hill to come back. Sweat dripped down the middle of my back. Several minutes passed. I read another story. Fifteen minutes. Twenty. I ran out of extra activities to keep the class busy. The kids were talking and getting rowdy. This wouldn't look good.

She *didn't* come back. My supervisor didn't come either. I finally did the lesson just for the kids. We talked about shapes. We counted the angles and sides of each treat. I completed the shapes comparison chart I'd made. I gave my closing sentence.

"And now we know the attributes of triangles, squares, and circles."

It was over. No one evaluated my skills, reviewed my carefully written lesson plans, or even attended my lesson with me while I dripped scared sweat on the kids. All my preparation, emotional energy, the college credit I'd worked for, seemed wasted. I'd practiced through the night for nothing. Well, maybe not nothing. Except for Jared, the kids thanked me for the snack.

My supervisor told me later that Mrs. Hill had cornered her in the hallway and demanded that I be removed from her classroom, immediately. Mrs. Hill said it was her job to "weed me out" of teaching.

My supervisor disagreed. I had passed all my courses with perfect grades. I was teacher material and not in need of weeding out. Yet Mrs. Hill refused to allow me back in her classroom.

With the kids at recess, the three of us sat in Mrs. Hill's room to decide my fate. The day, I'd only brought stale graham crackers for lunch—*the day Mrs. Hill decided to pull her weeds*. The hard plastic of a tiny chair cut into my back.

"Do you want to finish the program, or do you just want out?" the supervisor asked.

"I can't believe you're giving her the choice." Mrs. Hill glared. "There's no place for her in the teaching profession!"

Her words were an open palm to my bare face. *I should be angry!* I thought, but I was too numb to answer her insult. I could just quit, and all the disasters would stop—the tornado inside would let me go. But I'd already put so much of myself into getting to this point. All my life I'd dreamed of being a teacher. I'd given up most of my boy's early years. I'd spent so much family money, so much time doing homework.

If I quit, it would all be for nothing. I'd have to go home—not to my parents this time, but to my *husband*, the man who thought the world of me—and say, "Thanks for believing in me, but I won't be a teacher, after all."

That could not happen.

"I'd like to finish."

"Where do you want to student teach, then?" asked my supervisor. "Maybe I can get you reassigned. Another school might take you, since you only have nine weeks left."

Mrs. Hill stared, silent, daring me to become a teacher. She knew my fear: I wasn't good enough and probably never would be. I had nothing more for her to take, but I wouldn't give her my future.

I looked her right in the eye and gave the name of the school she hated.

"I'll go to Owen Charter."

I drove home, covered in humiliated sweat, and took off the skirt I'd been wearing. It was my favorite—soft and floral. Flowers and weeds. I balled it up and threw it in the dumpster. That skirt would never touch me again.

I put on some old pajamas and called my regular doctor. I'd worked at the mental health clinic and didn't want to be one of their patients. Still, I couldn't continue student teaching without medical help of some kind.

I got an appointment that afternoon. When I explained what happened to me, Dr. Ford nodded.

"Look what you've done to your brain. By letting anxiety escalate into panic, you've trained your brain to shut down in stress. No wonder you're passing out. You can have a little Lexapro until your brain heals."

She agreed to prescribe it for only one year to give me time to build some coping skills. After that, I would be on my own. Dr. Ford smiled and promised I'd begin to feel better in several weeks. It sounded like an eternity.

Meanwhile, I had to go to Owen Charter. I could only imagine the horrors that waited for me there. *I'll go to Owen Charter.* I didn't want to go to some "trashy" school. I'd only requested it to spite Mrs. Hill.

****

My new mentor teacher, Mrs. Gardener, was waiting at her desk when I arrived at Owen Charter the next morning. She took both my hands in hers.

"No matter what," she looked me right in the eye, "*you* are going to be a teacher."

She bowed her head and said a blessing for peace to come over me. Then her aide silently offered me an orange gummy bear, warm in her hand. I accepted.

Mrs. Gardener was a red-headed, smiley, singing person. She had time for kids, cats, friends, stories, cupcakes and phone calls—and student teachers who got themselves fired. Or, as my supervisor instructed me to say if anyone asked, "My previous placement was terminated."

Technically—since I wasn't being paid, I couldn't be fired.

Mrs. Gardener did lots of art projects—sticky things with puddles of real white glue—not rigid, heartless glue sticks. She let the kids talk a little, and they talked to me.

"I love you, Mrs. M. Can you come to my house for dinner? We're having macaroni and cheese tonight. You can sit by me, and my little brother can sit on the couch with our dog."

Mrs. Gardener's room was stinky, in a pleasant, kid sort of way: dirty necks and cherry Chapstick, peanut butter and jelly with sweaty sneakers. Downy fabric softener.

She let me teach small bits at a time until I was more comfortable than I'd ever been in front of people. Not one of her students tripped me. I never once passed out, and the nagging sizzle of anxiety quieted to a whisper. She reminded me every day that I was good with children.

"If you weren't called to be a teacher, the desire would have left you long ago. You're in the right place, doing the right thing with your life."

When needed, Mrs. Gardener worked as the school counselor. She was calming in that way for me, too. My regular doctor hadn't recommended that I see a therapist, but I interacted with Mrs. Gardener on a daily basis. She was a dose of soothing salve on a raw, skinless spirit.

Rather than feeling like the sideshow freak of Mrs. Hill's room, I fit at Owen Charter. Mrs. Gardener nurtured me until I was ready to take my own classroom of first graders.

I was no longer a weed to be plucked. Teaching was a savory stew, and I was one of the spices.

4
Let's Take Off Our Clown Wigs

Owen Charter School wasn't the type of "trash" that Mrs. Hill described, but it *was* a little different. An old Motel 6 had been converted into classrooms with chalkboards, coat hooks, and tile floors. The playground and sandbox covered part of the old parking lot, and an auditorium was under construction. On occasion, men and stray pit bulls slept in the bushes.

More than once, Principal Owen put the school in lockdown and confined students and teachers to their assigned classrooms, for exciting happenings in the neighborhood. Sometimes it was fairly harmless, like a swarm of bees escaping the dumpster. Sometimes it was worse; a man sitting in a rusted car, bleary-eyed, and watching our six and seven-year-olds play on the swings.

The charter program, created by Principal Owen, featured a special way of teaching children to read. She'd drawn happy little creatures called "Owen Pals" on hundreds of worksheets, and primary teachers were to present several a day. Principal Owen recorded CDs of catchy little songs that went with the alphabet sounds.

I liked the school. There was *time* at Owen Charter. With Mrs. Hill in public school, the day was so regimented that it flew by with hardly a second to enjoy the kids. At Owen, the day was longer, but fun.

Each teacher seemed to have a special identity. Mrs. Gardener sang and danced during lessons, and Principal Owen walked through the school wearing funny hats. Another teacher kept a hairy puppet on her hand and talked to it. I wasn't brave enough to be that much of a character. I was just plain old me.

For Christmas, I received my Arizona state teaching certificate. My mother gave me an antique slate and a set of *McGuffey's Eclectic Readers*—the kind Laura Ingalls Wilder used as a girl and as a teacher. They were so beautiful, so deliciously worn. I wanted to line up some dolls and a chalk board and use the books to play school again. Turned out, I didn't have to.

After everything I'd been through, I was scared to leave Owen Charter when student teaching was over. I loitered, then volunteered, then got up the nerve to substitute for absent teachers. The constant change made my heart pound, but I liked having Mrs. Gardener nearby.

"You keep showing up," she told me. "We'll keep putting you to work."

Late that spring, Principal Owen announced she was looking to hire a first grade teacher for the next school year and invited me to perform a "dog and pony show" for her.

I knew exactly what she meant. The dog and pony show was an exaggerated, colorful kids' activity, used to evaluate current teachers and interview new ones. In teachers' college, we learned to write a fancy ten-page lesson plan. It began with a "hook," an excited announcement that told the children what they would be learning. An outline detailed the steps the teacher would present. The closure reminded the children what they learned. Independent practice was something fun the kids could use to try out their new knowledge. The plan ended with a long list of materials, most of it purchased with the teacher's own money.

I was still recovering from the whole *being-fired* experience of student teaching at the other school, so my performance had to be stunning.

To prepare, I wrote a funny recipe story called "Oatmeal Cookies with Everything," and I included oversized props: a huge green plastic tub for a mixing bowl, a tennis racket for stirring. I mixed *everything* into the oatmeal cookies; a stuffed duck, a large fly, a bottle of Try-Harder Spray that I invented myself (and still wish I could patent). I practiced until three o'clock in the morning several times in a row and had the entire thing memorized to perfection. At the last minute, I made myself a chef's hat. I had an adorable show.

I was subbing that week for a teacher who was out ill, so I could borrow her classroom and students.

The morning of my observation, I prepared the children, meaning I *lied* to them. Mrs. Gardener, always my teaching buddy, told me the best way to get kids to cooperate was to tell them that Principal Owen was coming to see how quiet they could be.

I was standing in front of the class, answering "why" questions and arranging all my props, when Principal Owen walked in, wearing a curly green clown wig. I wasn't sure if she was marking her territory or making me welcome. Maybe both.

With the change in schools, I felt I had stepped out of the shark-infested water and into the circus. At Owen Charter, quirks were not only acceptable—they were encouraged by example. In fact, no one seemed to notice my nervousness, unless I confessed to it. I was home. I could figure out how to be a teacher here.

When the kids' laughter died down, I began.

"Good morning, Mrs. Owen. Thanks so much for coming to our class today. I'm sure you'll enjoy the lesson I prepared for you."

Then I spoke to her as I would a child.

"Let's take off our clown wigs and get started!" Thankfully she did, and the class's attention turned to our activity.

I put on my chef's hat and performed my "Oatmeal Cookies with Everything" story. It went off without a hitch. At the end, for independent practice, I showcased my bottle of Try-Harder Spray. Then I gave each student a small box of apple juice, which I'd covered in yellow construction paper ahead of time. I asked them to label their new product, an ingredient for their own "Cookies with Everything."

"Does anyone want to tell us about the product they invented today?" I asked, hoping someone would make me proud in front of Principal Owen.

One little boy, whose mother had done jail time, smiled and raised his hand.

"I'm going to call my product 'Why Are You Crazy?' because of my mother."

I was hired.

The following school year, I would become Owen Charter's new first grade teacher. I spent a good part of the summer making my classroom warm and welcoming, the tang of lemon bleach wipes in the air. I read lots of books for teachers about setting up an effective classroom, and mine was cute! Perfectly handwritten name tags on the desks, a shiny new alphabet on the wall, several hundred gently-used picture books, bought with my own money. Multi-cultural puppets, so politically-correct and lined up on the shelf. A grade book and a lesson planner on my desk, next to a copy of the state standards. A fresh box of bright yellow chalk was a nod to that little girl I'd once been.

I'd decided to go by "Mrs. M." My last name was not one that the kids pronounced easily. I was still rattled, but I had a place to go and a nice name to answer to—a name with potential. Like a too-big shirt, the name gave me room to grow, to wiggle, or to quake. I might not have been a character like the other teachers at Owen Charter, but I was building a good reputation and I had my Mrs. M-ness.

5
Then She Soiled

After a lifetime of dreaming, years of college, months of practice, weeks of preparing the room—it was finally my first day of school. Today was here. I was a teacher in my own classroom. My stomach felt jittery, but they were happy jitters.

I woke up early, showered and curled my hair, set my make-up with a little powder and ate a good breakfast. I'd ironed a new flowered skirt the night before. I was ready. I had everything. My dream of being a teacher had come true. It was here for me to live it and breathe it every day.

Once at school, I stood alone in my classroom, admiring its beauty one last time. Mrs. Gardener came in to give me a hug. I needed nothing more, except my students.

At eight-thirty that morning, while I was busy smiling and taking attendance and putting names to faces, little Monica ran out of the bathroom, screaming. Naked, she threw her green scissors across the class. The other children watched, stunned and silent, until a girl cried.

"She hit me with her scissors!"

I stood motionless for a moment, feeling my love of teaching drain from me. I had a psychology degree as back-up. I should have known what to do, but nothing magic came to mind. Monica continued to run, scream and grab things she could throw.

I flung open the adjoining door to Mrs. Gardener's first grade room.

"I need help in here!"

Mrs. Gardener saw the nude flash of Monica and called over the school paging system.

"Attention all staff: Mrs. M. needs immediate help in first grade. Immediate help to Mrs. M.'s room!"

I blocked Monica from running out the door.

A couple of office ladies, eyebrows high and lips tight, arrived and wrestled Monica into a towel. They carried her skinny, thrashing body out of my room. An aide grabbed her clothing from the bathroom floor and ran after them.

Heidi, a freckly little red-headed girl who was missing her front teeth, sat in the back of my class.

"I don't like that new naked girl," she said.

Neither did I.

Later that morning, the aide phoned with an update.

"It took three adults to hold your little Monica down and get her dressed. Then she soiled."

Soiled was school-talk for "shit herself."

While my students went to recess, I tried to call Monica's parents to let them know something was terribly wrong. The cell and home numbers were disconnected. I tried the father's work number, which belonged to a coffee shop in the mall.

"Hello, I'm looking for Mr. Walker. This is Mrs. M. from his daughter's school."

"I don't know a Mr. Walker," his coworker answered. "I don't know why you'd be calling here."

I found out later Mr. Walker certainly *did* work at that coffee shop and was likely there when I called. His coworkers had long been trained to get teachers off the phone quickly. Owen Charter wasn't Monica's first school.

After lunch, Principal Owen escorted Monica back to my class and left. The child was on my roster. I was now responsible for her, no matter what. Scowling, Monica crouched under her desk. After our morning, I was tempted to do the same.

Monica wouldn't color a picture. She wasn't interested in hearing me read a picture book with funny rhymes. She didn't want plastic counting bears to hold or even throw at others. Her outbursts and screaming continued, but at least she kept her clothes on. Somehow, the class and I made it through the afternoon.

The second morning, I walked my line of students into our class.

"Good morning, boys and girls," I greeted them in a pleasant teacher voice. "Please find your desks, just like yesterday."

"Just like yesterday" was the wrong thing to say. This time Monica pulled off her shoes and threw them. She yanked my precious library books off the shelves and dumped them in the trashcan. She climbed onto the drinking fountain and leaped over the heads of two students sitting nearby. She kicked over a desk, hit a child with his own ruler, and then ran to the bathroom and slammed the door.

When I'd dreamed of teaching, it wasn't like this!

I opened the bathroom door and found Monica hiding between the wall and the toilet, naked again. She screamed, so I quickly backed away and left her there. From my experience working at the mental health clinic, I knew it would be risky to be alone with this child. I was afraid she might accuse me of things someone else seemed to have done. I let her stay in the bathroom until morning recess, reasoning that the other students needed a teacher too.

My class seemed confused. Apparently, first grade wasn't going the way they'd imagined either. Quiet and well-behaved, they worked hard to please me. I loved them for that. We were in the Monica trenches together. My class management skills were good, but nothing seemed to work with Monica. I imagined mean Mrs. Hill, sneering at me.

"I told you that you'd never be teacher!"

At dismissal that day, I pushed through the line of parents, cars, and kids and caught up with Monica and her mother.

"Mrs. Walker?" I called out.

She turned away from me.

"Mrs. Walker!"

She paused at her car door, keys in hand. Mounds of McDonald's trash covered the floorboards. That in itself did not alarm me. People had different standards, and teachers couldn't call Child Protective Services on every dirty car. I kept trying.

"Mrs. Walker, I need to talk to you. Monica has been screaming and throwing things."

"Really?"

Then she turned to Monica.

"Well, honey, after a day like that, we'd better get you some ice cream to cheer you up!"

Tossing Monica into a booster seat, she drove away.

Something was wrong here. I was *responsible* for this child, for lots of children, and Monica's own parents were making it harder for me.

All that first week, my stomach hurt, though not in the impending doom way of Mrs. Hill. I feared Monica only as I would a spider to be squashed. Every day, I wished her out of my room.

Each morning on the drive to school, angry tears ran down my face. I steered with one hand and wiped tears with the other. I chewed a double dose of Tums. I growled in frustration until I parked and opened the car door.

Why was this happening to me, of all the first grade teachers in town? I had worked so hard for the opportunity. If anyone deserved to be a teacher, it was me. That child could have been enrolled anywhere. She didn't need to ruin my class, my career.

My old powerlessness with Mrs. Hill somehow intertwined with Monica. In my nighttime dreams, the two had morphed together—Mrs. Hill's blonde bob on tiny Monica. Monica at a large desk, saying, "You'll *never* be a teacher!" And big Mrs. Hill running naked through my classroom.

I wanted to feel like a successful teacher who was at peace with life and competent in my skills. I recalled my years in preschool—surely there was *some* experience I could draw from. We'd had our share of marathon criers and kids who peed places they shouldn't. But those kids were just slightly older than toddlers. That sort of behavior went with the territory. None of them compared to Monica.

I took a deep breath and swallowed hard as I entered my classroom each morning. I hadn't let Mrs. Hill take away my dream, and I wouldn't let Monica. I would get out my bottle of Try-Harder Spray. I finally had a teaching job—a real chalkboard—and I refused to let a child make me dread my days.

But after the second week of school, I was whipped. I went to my teaching buddy, Mrs. Gardener, who was my human map into the world of teaching.

"I know it's early in the year, but I have this little girl, Monica. I don't know what to do with her."

"This is your naked kid?"

"Yeah. Can you come and observe her for a while?" I begged.

"You betcha," she nodded. "I'll come this morning while my class is at recess." Her assessment took only a couple of minutes. Monica performed at her best, throwing books and screaming.

"She's done this every day," I said.

Mrs. Gardener gave me some paperwork to fill out.

"We need her diagnosed and in Resource Education services as soon as possible."

I was relieved someone knew what to do.

Initial tests suggested that Monica might have had an emotional disability, but Monica's mother had trouble showing up to our requested parent meetings. Until she did, there was nothing much we could do. Meanwhile, the behavior continued.

Under Arizona's failure-to-report laws, teachers were required to report concerning behavior, and we did. But Monica's tantrums went on.

Consequences did not matter to her. She didn't care if she lost her daily sticker or had to miss recess and stand by the building, watching the other kids play. She didn't care if she had to do her work alone in the classroom with me. She *loved* to write "I will keep my scissors to myself" ten times. Monica relished in-school suspension, and she liked having an aide to herself.

I tried rewarding her for short periods of cooperation in the classroom. I rewarded her for finishing a math paper or a positive attitude. I let her choose something from a special prize box, full of sparkly pencils, or I gave her five minutes of extra recess.

Monica was willing to one-up every consequence and reward I had. Nudity and soiling always won. I became aware of a recurring thought in my head.

I hate teaching!

This couldn't happen. I deliberately put it away from me. I *didn't* hate teaching, I hated dealing with this child's behavior.

I was desperate. Mrs. Gardener suggested we say a blessing over Monica's desk each morning before school. Some days it helped, and some days it didn't.

After several weeks, I began to know Monica as a person and not as a pain in my ass. She loved the color pink, and so did I. She ate bacon for breakfast, she told me between screams, her breath a smoky reminder. She hated tight clothes, which was a feeling I could identify with, although I kept mine on.

Eventually, whether I liked Monica or not, I needed to teach the rest of the class. I was able to get time without Monica in the room by presenting my grade book to Principal Owen.

"Look at these spelling scores, Mrs. Owen. When Monica is in my classroom, the grades drop below a C for every single student. When Monica is in suspension or absent, more than half of the students score 100 percent."

"We can't have this, Mrs. M. Is it because you're new to teaching and you have poor classroom control?"

Her question was a punch to the gut, but she was my principal. She had a right to know. Secretly, I'd wondered if Monica's behavior *was* my fault. I wondered if Mrs. Hill had been right about me, that I wasn't cut out for teaching. But I decided that Principal Owen wasn't familiar with my class management, and she simply wanted to end the child's bizarre behavior.

"No, Mrs. Owen," I assured her. "The rest of the students in my class are perfectly well-behaved. Walk in anytime."

"I'll do that, Mrs. M. We may need to put her in an experienced teacher's room. That's probably all it would take to calm her down."

I could see the question in her eyes. *Was incompetence the reason I'd been fired from student teaching before?* This was a direct challenge from Principal Owen. Tears burned behind my eyes, but I refused to let them fall.

As much as I wanted Monica's shrieking fits out of my classroom, I couldn't let Principal Owen reassign her to another teacher. It would announce my failure to the whole school. I'd be branded, and possibly not offered a contract for the next year. Besides, I had a couple things in common with the monster child, and that felt like progress.

Principal Owen was not ridiculing my anxiety, not bullying. She was only asking that I do my job. For that, I was grateful.

"Mrs. Owen," I said firmly, loudly, so she could not mistake my words. "I am a teacher. I will teach *all* the students on my roster. That includes Monica."

Principal Owen paused, looked me over and nodded. It was more of a graduation, a turning of my tassel, than I'd had from the college. I felt myself swell with pride and shake with terror at the same time.

After three schedulings, we met with Monica's mother for an individual education plan, an IEP meeting at eight o'clock on a Friday night. Principal Owen discreetly asked about past behaviors, but Monica's mother denied any knowledge of them. Just to be on the safe side, Mrs. Gardener would counsel with Monica weekly.

We arranged for Monica to complete my classwork in a separate room with a resource teacher, where the rest of us couldn't hear her scream. I felt better that my entire class would receive an education. Monica would too.

Even in a separate area, Monica's violent outbursts continued. I was relieved. It wasn't me, after all.

"This kid is like breaking a horse!" Principal Owen said.

She purchased a school-wide course in crisis prevention and physical take-down methods for use on out-of-control children, and she had an isolation room built.

One day, Monica's morning aide called me to the self-contained room. It was eerily empty. The paint was scratched down to bare wooden beams. Holes vaguely shaped like the heels of little Mary Janes marred the drywall.

"Did she do this?" I asked.

I knew the aide watched Monica vigilantly.

"She did in the time it took me to pee."

"Holy crap!" I said. "Have they considered an exorcism?"

"She's doing three days of suspension at home while the school rebuilds the room and installs video cameras."

When Monica returned, I brought the day's assignments to her. She now sat under video supervision.

"What's going on today, Monica?"

"Well, I have a temper, but it kind of left me for now."

She seemed so calm and adult in her own insight.

"Monica, I like you this way. Can you try to get your work done more often?"

She turned her pixie face to me and smiled. There was a sweetness about her when she wasn't screaming.

The self-contained room and intensive supervision of the video camera seemed to soothe her. I wished she would behave as well in a classroom.

Halfway through the year, which was about the time we learned to manage Monica, to predict her rough days, to recognize a look on her face that indicated imminent violence, Monica's parents pulled her out of Owen Charter. According to her records, she'd been withdrawn from a couple of other schools in kindergarten as well.

When she left, I wondered if the next teacher would be as shocked as I had been or if someone "experienced" would know what to do. A few days later, I received an urgent phone call.

"Hi, Mrs. M. My name is Mrs. Sharp. I teach at Lowell Elementary. I have a former student of yours, Monica Walker. You don't happen to have any valid phone numbers or know of a way I can reach her parents, do you? I can't get her to stop screaming."

"I'll give you the dad's work number at the mall," I told her. "Keep trying it, and eventually one of his coworkers will give in."

Student history is confidential, of course, but teachers talk off the record.

"And, Mrs. Sharp—if Monica screams in the bathroom, she's probably naked. Don't go in there alone."

"I understand, Mrs. M. Thank you so much."

It seemed teachers' college had left a lot out of our training. There was barely enough time in the program to cover math, reading, writing and the state standards.

Teacher textbooks did not include a chapter on screaming nude children who destroy a pretty classroom.

I tried not to let it get to me. It was just my first year. I'd worked hard to earn the job, pined for it all my life, fought Mrs. Hill for the right to teach and won. I thought about all the money I'd spent on earning my certificate and then on furnishing the classroom. One student could not ruin that for me. Monica was only temporary, but teaching was my own horse to break. And I would. I was nervous, not wimpy. I replayed the moment Principal Owen had looked me up and down and found me—not *unsatisfactory*, but good enough.

6
Two Kids Enter, One Kid Leaves

I decided to give it a chance. Teaching could grow on me. I loved showing kids how to read, and first grade was all about reading. I related to the kids who feared it; learning new skills scared me, too. But reading had so many uses. It was my private escape from sticky social trouble. Reading was independence and power. My mission in life was to help my students love it too.

I'd had my own troubles as a child when I learned to read.

****

My mother wore blue polyester pants, a gingham blouse, and a bouffant hairdo. She smelled like the pink lady powder in our bathroom that I wasn't allowed to touch. I was newly five years old and eye level with the elastic in her waistband.

"Let's walk up and register you for kindergarten," she announced one day. She seemed to know what she was talking about, so I accepted her hand and went along.

"Will there be kids?" I asked, as my mother opened the huge double doors of the neighborhood school.

"Lots of kids, the more the merrier."

It was merrier for her; she wouldn't be attending kindergarten. Meeting new people made my tummy feel funny.

My teacher was waiting at the door to her classroom. She was young for a grown-up, and blonde.

"I'm Miss Hyatt," she told me.

She knelt down and winked at me slowly, exposing purple eye shadow. This made me uncomfortable because my mother didn't wink, ever, and her eyelids were the same color as the rest of her.

Miss Hyatt used a stick pin—a stick pin!—to attach a pink paper kangaroo to my shirt. My mother pinned a matching mama kangaroo with a pouch to her own blouse. The kangaroos had some scribbling on them— our names, although I couldn't read them at the time.

Then my teacher gave us a tour of her classroom: tables and chairs, a wooden play kitchen, a wooly rug with bins of building blocks, and a picture book library. I wanted to pull up a bean bag chair and start learning to read, but then I saw the chalkboard and yellow chalk.

Yellow chalk!

While Miss Hyatt was busy talking to my mother, I grabbed the chalk and bit off a piece with my front teeth, just to be sure. *Smooth.* I was hooked.

To get ready for kindergarten, I got bigger shoes, longer pants and a bad case of bronchitis. The wet cough hung on, and my mother kept me home for the entire month of September.

By the time Miss Hyatt led me into her afternoon kindergarten, there were fully-formed social cliques and catty girl-rules that I didn't understand. Being shy and now late, it would have been better for me to start kindergarten the following year.

But in the '70s, kids weren't retained. They *flunked.* And no parent wanted to raise a failure. Besides, my mother had seen me playing school alone so much, she thought it was time I met other children.

Two of my classmates, Cynthia and Kimberly, wore ribbons in their hair, and dresses. They glared at my home-sewn shirt and pull-on corduroys.

"You can't sit by us."

I quietly accepted their shooing away and moved to another table. As the baby in my family, I was used to this sort of treatment, and these girls spoke with authority. I had long been suspicious of grown-ups because they often lied, but now I didn't trust kids either. There were just too many of them, and they all seemed to be in charge of me.

A few days later, Miss Hyatt read the names of some students who were needed in the office right away. I wanted to be one of the special kids whose name was on a list only the teacher could read, someone who was a little more important than Cynthia and Kimberly.

"Carrie," called Miss Hyatt. "And Brian."

He was the freckly boy who sat next to me in class. The teacher read several other names, too.

"Please go see the nurse."

When we arrived in a huddle, the nurse held out a tray.

"Carrie and Brian take a red sugar cube and eat it."

I could hardly believe my good fortune. At home, I got in trouble for eating the sugar cubes. I lifted my hand but hesitated.

"It's okay," the nurse smiled. "Take it."

The treat was sweet, crunchy, and dripping with a cherry-color sauce. The polio vaccine. The other kids were taken into the nurse's office and given shots. I could hear them crying. Sometimes it was better *not* to be on a list.

Back in class, Brian puked his ham and cheese sandwich and polio vaccine all over my new yellow shirt.

It was a real store-bought shirt from K-Mart too, and now it smelled.

Miss Hyatt rinsed it out in the classroom sink and let it dry by the window while I sat at the table in my undershirt. Cynthia and Kimberly smirked.

"Baby clothes. She's wearing *baby* clothes."

I didn't know what to say to that, so I looked away.

Miss Hyatt spoke to the class.

"Be on your best behavior."

Then she left the room to take queasy Brian to the nurse. Back then, teachers often left the kids completely unattended to chat with a teacher across the hall, to run to the bathroom, or to get something from the office. The worst thing any of us did without adult supervision was to run around and laugh a lot. Someone might have thrown a chalky eraser, someone named Cynthia.

As time went on, I noticed that Cynthia and Kimberly also had dibs on the little wooden kitchen. And whenever they asked her to, Miss Hyatt would play *This Old Man* on the piano. Certain others did not get to use the little kitchen, and Miss Hyatt would not play the piano for them. This seemed unfair, but I didn't have the vocabulary to question it.

Back then, teachers didn't have to worry about "fair" because the best and the strongest were supposed to come out on top. It was natural selection in the kindergarten thunder dome: Two kids enter, one kid leaves. I was too big to hide and too small to compete; maybe that was why I'd received the kindergarten-issue stick pin.

There seemed to be a secret language that only strong people knew. I couldn't read or write or even hit. I felt mute and armless. It was not my fault. Kids my age grew up with very few TV programs to copy behavior from.

In my family, it was *Sesame Street* and *Hee Haw*, or *Lawrence Welk*, if the static cleared. Smooth dancing Lawrence Welk, with his heavy hair grease, would hardly have balled up his fist or used cross words with a pair of singing twins.

After watching Miss Hyatt, I decided that teachers were strong. They knew the secret language and understood the TV programs. They were in charge of the kids, rather than being at their mercy, like I was. If *I* were a teacher, kids couldn't tell me to leave their table or refuse to let me use the wooden play kitchen. If *I* were a teacher, I could choose the songs and read the lists.

I tried hard that year to learn my alphabet letters, but my parents wouldn't help me with reading.

"That's your *teacher's* job," they insisted.

The next year, I went to first grade. Mrs. Baxter's room was not a pleasant learning environment either. I worked up the nerve and asked her for help.

"Mrs. Baxter, those boys are taking things out of my desk."

I pointed toward the ransacking. I'd brought small, stuffed animals and doll blankets and set up a bed for them in a corner of my desk; they were friends I could count on. I kept a pet rock in my pencil tray, and a picture of my mom clutching her purse for days when the separation anxiety left me quivering.

"Well, if you don't like it, make them stop."

I had no idea how to *stop* another child. My mother had similar expectations of me. She'd twisted my ear once for allowing a neighborhood girl to break all my crayons in half. It had made sense to me—if the crayons were broken, we'd both have a purple to use. No taking turns, no ugly negotiating.

"You should have stopped her," my mom said.

I was years away from influencing others, but thankfully, reading came looking for me. And with it, a rich and entertaining thought life. One day, Mrs. Baxter sent us all to our desks and told us to turn to a page in our phonics book. She read some directions for us.

"Write the names of two drinks."

I was used to my parents tricking me into things. They insisted broccoli was yummy and that shots wouldn't hurt. There was something sneaky about Mrs. Baxter too. She might not tell us what we really needed to write in the book. She might even *lie*.

Kathy, who sat in front of me, was a more reliable source. She told me to write down what I ate for breakfast. That seemed reasonable, so I wrote, "pancakes."

I showed my book to Mrs. Baxter.

"You cannot drink pancakes. Kathy wrote the same answer. You should know better than to listen to her."

Cynthia and Kimberly laughed. I sighed. Somehow, I was responsible for my own wrong answer and also to know better than Kathy. First grade was a heavy weight about my neck. I returned to my seat and kept my eyes on the paper so long that I actually read the simple instruction at the top of the page.

I understood and trusted it completely. The written words did not come from a wily adult or a friendly girl. They were just for me on my page and clearly those directions knew what they were talking about. I wrote my answers: Coke, milk.

"You are one hundred percent right," said Mrs. Baxter.

I loved written words that day. Reading was *thinking*, and knowing for sure. I wanted to hear all those thoughts in my head. I could stand up for myself and protect what was mine with those words. Those words would back me up and make me right. It was my secret power. All I lacked was a cape.

There were four reading groups in Mrs. Baxter's first grade. She gave us a choice.

"Would you like to be called the 'Red Group' or the 'Blue Group?' We voted by raising our hands, and we chose red. I preferred blue and made my choice known, but I was outnumbered. Sometimes even secret powers didn't work out.

I noticed that each group used a different book, and that the Green Group used a particularly thin book. Those were the kids with dirty faces, whose pant legs didn't reach their ankles.

The Yellow Group used a very thick book, one I could never hope to read. Those were the snotty girls who played *Charlie's Angels* at recess and would later wear short skirts and sleep with football players. Cynthia and Kimberly were in the Yellow Group.

Our Red Group used a book with pictures of kids in pretty clothes, lots of fluffy kitten and ice cream mishaps, and words I could read myself, with a little sounding out. I didn't enjoy reading in front of other kids, though. When I was finally allowed to keep my book and take it home, I read it to shreds.

"I can read!" I told my mother one evening.

I sat on her step stool in the kitchen, poking her knee caps and listening to the chicken spatter in her pan.

"I'm cooking dinner now," she warned me.

So I got up and read to myself in the bathroom mirror. The words in books stayed comfortingly the same every time I read them. Words didn't try to trick me, and the girl in the mirror never laughed or got too busy.

I could be my own reading group, and I could name it anything I wanted. I could be the Teddy Bear Group or the Blankie Group or even the Super-Powered, Better-Than-Cynthia-and-Kimberly Group, and no one would know.

The first year I taught at Owen Charter, I didn't name my reading groups at all, although 'Demons' and 'Angels' would have been fun when Monica was in class. Even shapes and colors seemed to set up an unfair caste system. A thunder dome of sorts. And those kids would have seen right through it.

I figured it out 30 years ago, and I was only in the *Red* Group.

7

Glad I'm Not Your Bear

Teddy Bear Day was a popular February activity at Owen Charter, before the state standards mandated more math and other core subjects. Each first grader could bring a small, favorite bear from home.

"Something huggable, that can sit with you at your desk," I told my class.

My palms were sweaty just planning a day like that, managing a room full of kids with distracting toys. But since Monica was no longer enrolled and destroying property, I was willing to try. I brought extras for the kids who "didn't use" stuffed animals anymore. Principal Owen suspended the school toy policy for the day to allow bear companions on the playground and in the lunchroom.

I had a bear too. He was a giant—over five feet tall, warm brown and squishy soft, with a gentle expression. I'd bought him at the Goodwill on half-price day, steering him around in my shopping cart as his arms flopped over the sides.

"Do you live alone, sweetheart?" asked a white-haired shopper.

"I'm a teacher."

I smiled. I thought I might put the bear in my class library area, a cozy place for the students to curl up and read.

Unfortunately, my dog, Chester, adopted the bear the minute I got it home. He sniffed its ears, walked in a circle twice, plopped down in the bear's lap and fell asleep.

On the morning of Teddy Bear Day, I wrestled the bear away from my dog, vacuumed the loose hair off and jammed the bear into the front seat of my VW Bug. I drove to school with him as my passenger; I was a lonely-looking person with stuffed animal friends.

To haul him from my car to the classroom, I wrapped my arms around his waist and let his feet drag the ground. Teacher parking at Owen Charter was nearly a block away.

When I got to the classroom, the kids were thrilled.

"Do you sleep with that bear?" someone asked.

"Sure," I said. "All the time."

"What's his name?"

"Guthrie."

"Did your mom give him to you?"

"Yes, but I had to keep my room clean for a whole year."

I was making things up, but the kids didn't relate to married life. In truth, he was just my dog's bed and not quite clean enough for the class library.

Teddy Bear Day fell on a Friday, and I didn't have it in me to lug the bear back out to my car. My dog, Chester, had a deeper nesting bed that he liked to use on colder nights anyway, so I left the bear at school.

Our Arizona town received a rare snowstorm that night. All weekend, my family watched a heavy, wet snow decorate the yard.

On Monday morning, as I was drying off from my shower, I heard the phone ring. An odd sound so early in the day. I ran for it.

"Mrs. M., heads up."

Principal Owen was not who I'd planned on talking to while wrapped in a towel.

"You're going to want to come to school early, and wear old blue jeans and sneakers."

"Why?"

"The building leaked in that storm. Your classroom is under a couple of inches of water. I've called in some help."

I dressed fast, put my hair in a ponytail and took a Pop Tart with me to the car.

Principal Owen was right. My room was flooded, but only *my* room. School would not be cancelled. The giant bear had absorbed a good amount of water and was soaked from the neck down. A janitor was busy assessing the damage and wanted me to get the bear out.

I walked over to my teaching buddy, Mrs. Gardener's room, just as her light came on. She held her keys in one hand and her lunchbox and purse in the other, sunglasses still perched on her head. I smiled innocently.

"Can you help me with something?"

"Sure, whatcha need?"

She dropped her things on a chair and followed me to my classroom, where I pointed to the standing water and the soggy bear. The janitor was gone.

"Oh, forevermore! Days like this don't get better. You *know* that, don't you?"

I was hopeful.

"It'll work out."

Even with the two of us, the bear was too heavy to lift while he was dripping wet. We took turns, wringing him out, one body part at a time, inside the classroom, and we let the water gush onto the floor. Our shoes were already sopping.

I let Mrs. Gardener hold the bear's ears, because they were dry. I took his squishy feet, and we carried him down the block to my car. I didn't want the bear, also a wet dog bed, soaking the seats. I did some quick thinking.

Fortunately, the weather had turned sunny and windy after the snowstorm. I opened my car window and shoved the bear in, head first. His huge, brown butt and legs hung down the outside of the car and would dry in the sun.

"This seems like the best we can do for his stinky fur," I said.

"Glad I'm not your bear," she said, her shoes making squishy noises as she walked.

By the time I got back to the classroom, kids were lining up outside the door. The janitor was removing the standing water with a screeching shop vac. No teaching could be done in my room; it would be too loud and wet.

"I'll probably be out of here by lunchtime," he called out. "But I've got air blowers, too. You'll have your room back tomorrow."

"Tomorrow?" I asked. "Where am supposed to teach my class?"

"Hey, I'm just here to get this water out. I can't fix everything."

The kids waited in the doorway, looking at me. Most had morning hair and jam-smeared faces. I tried to think of options. All the other classrooms were occupied; it was a regular school day for them. The weather was sunny, but not warm enough to hold class on the playground. *What to do?* In my indecision, I could hear my heart beating. I reached for the phone.

"Principal Owen? This is Mrs. M. Where would you like me to take my students? We can't stay in my room today."

"Oh, I forgot about your water. There aren't any empty classrooms. Band is rehearsing in the new auditorium, and the art room is always busy. I guess *anywhere you can find some space* will be fine."

Mrs. Gardener offered me a corner in her room, but only some of my students would fit there. I wished I could find a spot, like the carpeted area at my old preschool, where we'd had "circle time" and stories.

"Okay, class. I have an idea!"

With first-year-teacher enthusiasm, I grabbed a stack of readers, dry from the shelf. I handed the can of pencils and several assignments to two of my more responsible students. Then I led the class upstairs in the new auditorium.

There was some floor space in the hallway by the bathrooms, where there was less noise away from the band rehearsal. It smelled of carpet glue and cleaning products. With the bathroom lights turned on, the spot was ideal for reading groups and an old-fashioned math circle, and maybe even a singing game if we had time.

The distractions kept my usual fluttery stomach calm. I felt competent and adult. I'd solved the relocation problem, and right in front of the kids, too. Teaching could continue.

Except, unlike the preschoolers—these students were used to sitting in desks, in carefully assigned rows, with several inches of personal space between them. Owen Charter used the traditional school seating chart. Without it, scuffles broke out and chatty best-friendships formed.

Arranging personalities was an art, and I was confident in it. This was a beginner skill they taught in teachers' college, using a poster board to represent a classroom and tiny sticky notes with names, more easily moved than desks.

I'd mastered the seating chart while student teaching in Mrs. Gardener's room. She called it "Musical Personalities." My own seating chart was fine-tuned, but not transferable to the oblong space of the auditorium bathroom hallway.

In the classroom, my front row was made up of kids who were low, academically. The students with individual education plans needed preferential seating. I put those kids in the front of our clump, with a couple of silent ones to separate the talkers.

The second row of kids gave up easily. I buddied them with excellent students for that day. The third row bunch were the good, responsible students. They paid attention from any distance. Even on the floor by the bathroom, I didn't have to tell them where to sit.

The last row in the classroom was made up of kids who drove everyone else crazy. They clicked pencils and hummed songs. I moved them onto the carpet, away from the echo and temptation to use the bathrooms.

Satisfied, I began the class with a flagless Pledge of Allegiance. Eager to get on with our lessons, I taped a large sheet of poster paper to the wall, so I'd have a place to write math facts with a bright marker.

"Class, let's…"

There came a pulsating shriek that made our ears ache—a fire drill, too loud to scream directions over. When we'd practiced fire drills in the classroom, we followed a specific evacuation plan: out a certain door, around a corner to the playground in two minutes. Kids were creatures of habit, and we were far from our usual route. I motioned everyone to follow me down the stairs, through the building, and along a sidewalk.

I'd brought my grade book and class roster with me—no teacher at Owen Charter would dare to be without them. Finally, we gathered on the playground with the rest of the school, timed and accounted for by Principal Owen.

"I thought we'd lost you, Mrs. M.," she mused, tapping her pencil on her clipboard.

I held up my grade book and roster to prove my worth.

"We're having class in the auditorium."

The fire drill absorbed another half hour of the day. *Crazy* was better than a screamer, better than cowering or student teaching with Mrs. Hill. The kids were strangely focused in the novel surroundings of the bathroom hallway, even after the fire drill. We got a lot of work done. I was proud of them and of me.

"That was the most fun day ever!" one of the girls exclaimed. "Can we always do math on the wall?"

"No." I smiled.

We'd probably never *have* to. A flooded floor, a wet bear, class in the bathroom hallway and a fire drill! What were the chances? I didn't even ask myself what else could happen—obviously anything in this job. I wasn't picky; I'd take a day without my stomach churning. I was letting go of my romantic version of teaching and accepting whatever came along.

After school, I walked to my car, half-expecting the giant bear to be gone, stolen, or poised on the roof of my car in a suggestive position. But he was there as I left him. His butt hung out the window for all to see, now dry and fuzzy, though still a little musty. I was pleased.

Owen Charter cancelled Teddy Bear Day after that to allow more time for core subjects, and I missed it. I soaked up the confidence like my bear had done with the water. It wasn't like me to accept events with no plan or fretting, but there was nothing else I could do. It was a tiny taste of the fun I dreamed of having as a teacher.

My dog was just happy to get his bear bed back.

8

Color on Your Own Paper, Hooker!

With Monica gone and my students settled in, I began to notice that school life was much different than when I was growing up. Even the rules that provided basic structure had changed.

In the '70s we had only one rule: *Don't kill each other.* We followed it, without much supervision. There were only a couple of aides on the playground to watch many classes of children, and each of us shy girls chose an aide's leg and hung on for protection. The rest of the kids were on their own unless something horrible happened.

One recess, I watched a brown-haired boy named Arnold go flying off the merry-go-round, land in the rocks and leak blood from his head. The whole thing reminded me of *Curious George*, the monkey who lived with his yellow-hatted poacher friend. George also had episodes of spinning on things, such as an old-time record player, and flying off, but without the blood.

My classmate, Arnold, lay on the ground where he fell, still and quiet and bloody. I hung onto the aide. I didn't care much for Arnold and wasn't alarmed. An older boy ran up.

"One of the little kids got hurt over there!" he yelled.

But the aide hadn't seen it, and adults were not required to believe children in the '70s. This didn't bother me. It was just the way adults were.

"Go play!" she told the boy.

She had two shy girls attached to her legs and hundreds of other children to watch. She didn't tolerate tattling.

"He's *bleeding!*"

The aide blew her nose on a hanky she'd pulled from her pocket. Gently pushing us girls from her legs, she ambled over to Arnold and saw the pooling blood. Eventually, the new school nurse, a crabby lady with cold hands, who didn't want to hear complaints, came out and picked Arnold up, rather roughly. I waited for her to announce, "It's his own fault," as grown-ups so often did. Then we shy girls gathered at the chain link fence and watched as the nurse drove away with him in her personal car.

She brought him back to class later the same day with his newly-shaved scalp sewn up in black stitches, and wearing the same blood-spattered T-shirt. I felt sort of sorry for Arnold then; I thought he should have at least gotten an afternoon of cartoons at home for his trouble.

If this had occurred at Owen Charter, we'd have called 911 and sent the boy on a pricey ambulance ride to the emergency room. He'd have enjoyed at least a week of excused absences. The school might have been named in a lawsuit, and the merry-go-round removed from the playground, permanently. Not to mention the bloody T-shirt, which would be treated as if it contained blood-borne pathogens, and red-bagged for home.

At Owen Charter, we had tons of rules for the playground in cutesy phrases such as *No hanging from the Swiss cheese* and *No jumping from the spider*, both climbing structures for children. We had *swing counting*, a procedure where children who were waiting, counted backwards from one hundred to motivate the other students to end their turns peaceably. There was also a mandated safety ratio of aides to students.

Owen Charter teachers and playground staff were required to take any child-reported event seriously and investigate immediately. We supervised the interactions and even the *conversations* of children, to ensure appropriateness. We attended trainings on how to filter regular kid stuff from a potentially bullyish remark and perform interventions.

"A girl hit me at school today," I once reported to my mother.

"Hit her back!" was her immediate response.

Owen Charter students were taught never to hit, and to go directly to an adult for help. We coached timid children into friendships and defended them from cliques and bullying.

I wish a teacher had modeled assertive behavior for me the way I did for kids at Owen Charter. I like to imagine the adults in my life, having the insight and the patience to encourage me.

"Put your shoulders back. Look that Cynthia girl right in the eye. Go ahead! I won't let her hurt you. Now, say in your big voice, 'Don't hit me!'"

The little girl in me stands taller just thinking about it.

In the classrooms at Owen Charter, teachers posted indoor rules, with loopholes sewn up tight. I stole the rules that my teaching buddy, Mrs. Gardener, used. These rules were my security and made the behavior of most kids more predictable: *Follow directions the first time. Keep hands, feet and objects to ourselves. Work quietly and respect others.* They covered any wiggle room that clever, modern children tried to interpret.

When I was a kid, the class rules amounted to whatever the teacher said they were, and parents didn't know or care otherwise. If someone had asked my mother what the rules at school were, she would have said she had more important things to worry about, like selling Avon and leaving my father.

There is an imaginary pendulum in educational trends. I grew up with a couple of the trends myself: a back-to-basics approach was replaced by fancy math methods my parents couldn't help me with, and teachers replaced themselves with learning centers. I didn't like it, though. I felt like I had no adults to guide me.

Extreme parent involvement grew fashionable while I was teaching preschool in the early '90s. The new generation of parents was young and hip and no longer oblivious to the daily activities of their children. These people took a deep and personal interest in the rules at school, *and* in figuring out ways so that the rules would not apply to their children.

This felt unfair to me. I thought rules were as definite as the sun rising and setting. I'd followed the rules as a child, and it seemed today's kids should follow them too.

The trend continued at Owen Charter. The school created a formal list of classroom and playground rules that was signed by each parent and student as a matter of enrollment in an attempt to prevent arguments. One father, Mr. Roberts, had instructions for me.

"You are not to tell my boy 'no,' because it creates a negative environment for him. I want all the teachers to say in a gentle voice, 'Martin, it's time to be safe with your body.'"

I looked at Mr. Roberts, dumb-founded. What was the world coming to? I imagined myself speaking politely to Martin while he teetered at the top of the "Swiss cheese." I certainly wouldn't want to offend the child before he fell to his death.

Luckily for Martin, he was not adventurous. I never had to frighten him with "Get down! Now!" in my playground yell.

Many children today have enormous language abilities. In teachers' college, I was required to observe a public school kindergarten class. This was a rough group of five-year-olds. Several little girls were coloring pictures at a table. The chatter seemed happy and the colors bright. Suddenly, one little girl shoved another to the floor.

"Color on your *own* paper, hooker!"

Even as an adult, I was shocked. That remark would have gotten my mouth washed out with soap. My mother preferred the heavily-perfumed Avon soap in the shape of a green owl. It took hours to get the taste out of my mouth, and my only infraction had been to call my brother a "poop."

We had our share of potty mouths at Owen Charter too. Mrs. Gardener had an especially articulate student, Skyler. He was absent for a week, and she sent home his makeup work.

His mother hand-delivered the completed papers to Mrs. Gardener. On the top of the stack was a fill-in-the-blank work sheet:

Let's _____ and _____. Skyler created the sentence, "Let's <u>sit</u> and <u>fart</u>." Apparently, his mother hadn't checked his work before turning it in. Or then again, maybe she *had*. Mrs. Gardener returned the paper to Skyler's mother and requested that she help him write sentences appropriate for school.

Then the sentence crept its way into our adult conversations.

"Got any plans this weekend, Mrs. Gardener?"

"Yeah. Mike and I are gonna sit and fart."

****

That first year teaching, I noticed there were not only rules for kids but rules for us teachers too…a sort of teacher culture. Owen Charter was old school traditional: the teacher stood in front of the classroom, giving instruction, and the students sat in desks, ignoring her.

It had been the same when I was a child, until the second grade when my elementary school adopted a '70s hippie philosophy, with "pod"-style team-teaching. I sat for math and science in our homeroom with Mrs. Brown. Then, we kids walked to another room for spelling and reading, with a different teacher. But I liked Mrs. Brown, especially. She was chubby, laughed easily, and she came to my house to visit me. It was some kind of teacher rule that went with the new philosophy, and she visited every student's home at least once.

On the day she came, my mother cleaned the house, dusted and used the lemony furniture polish. Mrs. Brown rang our doorbell. All smiles and manners, we turned off the TV, even though *Happy Days* was on.

"Hello, Mrs. Brown. Please come in. Can I get you some tea?" my mother asked in her chatting voice.

Then my mother sent me to my bedroom, so they could speak privately. I pressed my ear against the crack under my door and lay still, hoping to hear how much everyone loved me.

"Your daughter is a good student," Mrs. Brown shared. "She's a nice girl, but she's shy and very quiet."

It's basically the same thing I hear today—me and any serial killer.

When the visit seemed to be winding down, I opened my door and timidly approached Mrs. Brown.

"Do you want to see my room?" I asked.

Kids always want to show people their rooms. As a teacher at Owen Charter, I got invited by first graders all the time to "come home with me and see my room." I kind of wished we'd had time for home visits; I'm sure they would have explained a lot. I often imagined the homes of children in my class: loving, but with loads of cats, or old and perfectly clean, or buried in a smelly hoard.

Mrs. Brown stood in the doorway as I plopped down on my bedroom floor.

"I don't have time to play," she smiled. "But your room looks very nice."

That was another rule followed by teachers and parents alike: *Adults did not play*. Playing was kids' business. Today, adults drop what they're doing and sit on the floor to play with children. Teachers of young children, myself included, were trained to kneel down at eye level when speaking to a child.

At the same time, we avoided touching the child in any way. We didn't want to put ourselves at risk for accusations. That seemed sad to me, and I did give very quick, chaste, pat-like hugs with one arm when kids asked for them.

One day, Mrs. Brown taught a science lesson on prehistoric life. She always had a good topic ready, which was another reason I loved her. We read some books and had some discussions. The best part was when Mrs.

Brown let us make dinosaurs out of clay, the squishy mud kind, that smelled like dirt and got on my face and in my hair.

I formed my blob of clay into a small garden lizard. But when the day came to apply glaze, my lizard was gone. I looked around, narrow-eyed, at my classmates, but I never saw who'd claimed it.

I accepted a leftover T-Rex and glazed that instead. My adopted dinosaur became beautiful under my loving hands. She was pink, with white polka-dots and black eyelashes. A real girl's dinosaur! Then she was sent away to be baked.

A few weeks later, Mrs. Brown returned them to us to take home.

"Keep the one you made, not the one you painted."

This time, my original lizard was found, painted a homely lead-gray by some grubby boy.

I didn't understand why I couldn't have my beautiful girl-dinosaur, the one I glazed, the one I loved. But there was a societal rule in the '70s, and Mrs. Brown followed it: *Adults didn't explain themselves to children.*

I finally hid the lizard in my lunchbox, ashamed that Cynthia and Kimberly might see him and think I'd chosen the hideous gray paint. I had that lizard well into my adult years, unable to stop hating him and unable to throw him away.

At Owen Charter, I made two teacher rules for myself: *Correct names were on all projects* and it stayed that way. And—I *did* explain to students some of my reasons for doing things, if it could help them understand. For example, "Why do we need fire drills?" students might ask.

"So kids don't burn up," was my honest answer, which also got immediate cooperation.

But it seemed to me that many Owen Charter parents explained themselves in dizzying detail to small children, showy and overdone. It took up my time while I waited for a parent who droned on.

"Courtney, Mommy gave you an apple in your lunch today, because we were out of oranges, but if you'll wait a couple of days until Mommy gets paid again, then we can…" and on and on.

Some days, I wished for a return to the '70s, when adults got the benefits of being adult, and kids were not catered to. But then there were other days when I wished I had been so important as a child.

During that first year of teaching, I tried to put the new playground and classroom rules into practice with this supercharged breed of kids who could think for themselves and argue their way out of a web of rules. I knew my dream of teaching was based on an antiquated model that had changed drastically over the last 30 years.

We were powerless little blobs of dinosaur clay back then, nothing like the miniature dictators kids are today. The kids I knew as a child might hit or pout or tattle, but they certainly didn't strip their clothes off and throw scissors in front of the new teacher.

Over the summer, I planned to look up some good teacher websites in order to find some books on classroom discipline. I wanted to practice projecting assertiveness like Cesar Milan in *Be the Pack Leader*. I figured that a pack of dogs was not much different than a roomful of kids. Summer would be a good time to work on it.

I ached to be competent and well-seasoned, knowledgeable and in control. All teachers were that way. It was some kind of new rule.

The Second Year

9
The New Strain

I kept telling myself that I'd had a rough first year with teaching, and my second year would be much better. I was now off the Lexapro, since Dr. Ford insisted I'd had enough time to build coping skills. Walking two miles a day took the edge off of my emotional build-up, as did getting more sleep than I had been. I determined that I wouldn't need to wear extra anti-perspirant or buy the economy size bottle of Tums anymore.

I was good to go that year: there were not two screamers in the world. Monica had to be the only one of her kind. I could teach first grade, Monica-free, for the rest of my career.

But that fall, I got Tyson. He was a stocky first grader, brown-eyed, with a military haircut. I met his family on Meet the Teacher night.

"Mrs. M., I'm Tyson's mother."

Mrs. Hammit shook my hand.

"My son hasn't done well at his last two schools. Principal Owen said that this school could straighten him out, and she encouraged us to enroll Tyson in your class. She says your teaching style would be good for him. I'm sure he'll do fine. Just be firm."

I wasn't sure I appreciated Principal Owen's vote of confidence, but it was an improvement over her doubts about me last year.

This time, I knew what to ask.

"Did Tyson have *behavioral* difficulties at his last two schools?"

I became aware of a screaming inside my head. This was post-Monica, and I could sniff out aggression like a cadaver dog. I wasn't sure I had the upper body strength to wrestle with this Tyson boy.

"Well no, not really." Mrs. Hammit shrugged. "I just didn't agree with their discipline policies."

"Okay. Then let me tell you about the expectations at Owen Charter."

We had procedures now and trained staff. I hated confronting this mother, but I knew it would prevent problems later. I described our rules for following directions and respecting others. I told her about our zero tolerance policy on hitting and rock throwing.

"In severe cases, we physically remove children who are acting out and put them in a small room for close monitoring, where they can't hurt anyone."

"Oh," his mother mumbled.

"I'll do my best to get him settled in at our school. Are you reachable by phone, Mrs. Hammitt?"

She said she was.

By the end of the first week, Tyson kicked three staff members, hard enough to leave large bruises, and gave two students black eyes.

My inner turmoil was different in that second year. The anxiety was specific and more refined. I was no longer terrified, shocked or ill-equipped to handle an aggressive child. Now, I knew what I was in for, and I dreaded it.

I immediately scheduled a meeting with the boy's mother and Principal Owen. We created a plan, and I set aside time every afternoon to discuss the day's behavior and consequences with his mother. My teaching buddy, Mrs. Gardener, set up counseling appointments with Tyson.

I used the school intercom to call for help so often, that Mrs. Gardener began teasing me. After school, when the kids were gone, she'd push the announcement button on her classroom phone.

"Bruises and black eyes are being given in Mrs. M.'s room. If you'd like a day off, please report to Mrs. M.'s room."

I stuck my head in her doorway.

"Thank you for that."

One morning, while getting my class from the playground, I watched Principal Owen walk by Tyson, who was playing in the sandbox. She was looking in the other direction. Tyson jumped on her, kicking and punching her to the ground. A child he'd hit recently screamed in empathy, but the others were too busy playing to notice. I was all she had.

"I've gotcha, Mrs. Owen!" I yelled.

Mrs. Gardener, who was also picking up her class, blew her whistle to get the other kids to safety.

Even as I was thinking that it served Principal Owen right for putting kids like Tyson in my class, I ran into the office to get her some help.

As a consequence, Tyson received multiple days of suspension and lost all recesses. His parents took him to a pediatrician, who prescribed medication. I was hopeful for a while, but I never saw much change in his behavior.

"I just don't like the idea of medicating my baby," his mother admitted to me during one of our daily phone calls. "I've only been slipping him a quarter tablet of the prescribed dosage, and I can hardly stand to do that."

I clenched my jaw. I was at a loss for what to say to this woman. Anything I could think of would be unprofessional. She knew she was putting teachers and children in danger. A sticky silence hung between us.

By the holiday season, I'd come to know Tyson well enough to predict and manage a lot of his behavior. I'd trained him to stay near me, so I could supervise him closely. A look in his eye or a refusal to do a spelling paper signaled that he'd punch a classmate soon if I didn't get him away from the rest of the kids.

"Come on, Tyson. Let's get you a drink of water. You'll feel better."

"Can I have a hug, Mrs. M.?"

"Can you do it without hurting me?"

"I think so."

Surprisingly, he was gentle with me, and I almost came to like him. When he suddenly punched yet another student, his parents had enough of Tyson being hauled to the self-contained room and pulled him out of school that same day. It was a good choice for everyone—an early Christmas gift, let's say.

"We're getting a lot more kids now who need counseling," Mrs. Gardener said, as we graded papers in her room.

"It's because we built that room for Monica," I told her. "It's calling to them."

Word did seem to get out that Owen Charter staff had experience with combative students. As a teacher, I believed that school readiness was more than just knowing the ABCs; it was being in control of one's own behavior.

The problem kids got a lion's share of my attention, anxiety and school services. The unfairness was frustrating. I wanted *all* my students to pay attention and learn to read. Why couldn't they just settle down and let me be their teacher?

I'd studied the basic human temperaments and child development stages for my psychology degree. I'd read Tracy Hogg's *The Baby Whisperer*, trying to figure out my own toddler's inclination to fuss. But it was more than that.

This was a new strain of child, a mutant strain, whose behavior made me feel poorly-matched for the classroom. I should have been born a big guy, with square muscles and a deadly glare—not a soft-spoken woman with a dream of working with kids. I was desperate to *manage* these students. There wouldn't be much teaching going on until I did.

I was still too high-strung to think on my feet. But given some time to stew and a little wiggle room, I could always come up with good ideas for next time. One of those ideas snuck up behind me and tapped me on the shoulder. *There were two kinds of kids, like the forces of nature.*

Some were the creative forces; they drew friendly pictures for people, they made pink flowers in art, they asked for tape to fix torn pages in library books, and they used their energy to build things up and make things better.

Other children were the destructive forces. They ripped the pages out of library books, they broke pencils and they used scissors to shred crayons. Not all these children had behavior problems; it was just their nature to tear down. Of course, I relished my time with the sweet, helpful ones, but my job was to teach all the kids in my class, whether they wanted to learn or not.

Placing them into categories felt empowering, muscular even. I wasn't victimized by these kids. I was the adult who could see around the corners they couldn't. I didn't need to be a big tough guy. Insight and problem-solving was my "deadly glare."

If I could somehow predict their disruptive behavior and perfect a way to handle it, then I could use the teaching techniques I paid for in college to educate these kids. I could *best meet the needs of the students*, which is the mission of all teachers.

Better still, I could stand in front of kids, any of them—the cooperative or the combative, and teach without feeling faint, seeing stars, or having trouble breathing. I bet myself that I could break those categories down even further and get control of my job!

10
First Grader Profiling

I started my profiles with Screamer characteristics, because Monica and Tyson had caused me the most hot tears and sleep loss. I created a computer file of proven strategies for Screamers: keep the child close to me, learn the facial expressions that precede behavior, call parents daily, keep Principal Owen involved, take one day at a time, document *everything*.

I also noted that I could prevent behavior by developing a rapport with the Screamers, as irritating as they could be. It helped to remember that some kids were a lot of fun, and some kids were going to prison.

In fairness, I thought of the pleasant students from good homes who earned above average grades, the creative forces in the classroom. They made me happy, but those kids didn't need profiling. I moved on to the ones that did.

****

The Humper: Carson was a quiet boy, blonde, chubby, in a well-cared for way. He paid attention in class and turned in his homework every day. He seemed to be nothing to worry about. But one day, during instruction, his face flushed and I heard a rhythmic *thumping* under his desk. I walked by to investigate. A multi-tasker, Carson had taken his penis out of his pants and was doing his business left-handed, so he could use his other hand to write.

I was shocked. I'd taken child development classes and was a mother myself. I understood that children have natural, innocent feelings as they grow up, but this was a *classroom*. There were other young students to consider.

I asked to speak with him at my desk.

"Carson, is there a problem with your pants?"

He shook his head.

"Is there something you need to take care of in the bathroom?"

"I don't think so." He shrugged.

"Okay, then. Let's keep the pants zipped and your hands on your desk when you're in class. Can you do that?"

He nodded and looked at his shoes.

Within seconds, however, there was the rhythmic thumping again. Now that I was aware of it, I heard it most of the time during class. Carson had been retained and was slightly older than the kids I was used to teaching. I spoke to a second grade teacher.

"No, second graders don't do that, either," said Mrs. Baker. "There must be a problem. I'd talk to the nurse."

I did. Her response was to sing the Van Halen song, *Hot for Teacher.*

"Very funny," I told her. "What should I do?"

"Well, sometimes kids have tight underwear, or itchy detergent gets them started digging around in there. Send him to me and I'll talk to him. And you should tell his mother to change laundry supplies and buy him bigger underwear."

I tried that, but the *thump, thump, thump,* continued. I moved him to the back of the room, away from the little girls he'd been sitting by. At least the other kids wouldn't see him.

I had no experience with children who did this sort of thing so openly and persistently. I worried that he might have been exposed to something sexual at home. Perhaps he had walked through the room when an older brother was watching a racy movie or something.

I called a conference with Carson's mother that included the school nurse and Principal Owen. We moved several little plastic chairs into a circle and sat down.

"Mrs. Sanders, I wanted to speak with you because…"

Oh geez! How was I supposed to say it? I squirmed, making a mental note to practice difficult conversations ahead of time. Finally, I just said it.

"Mrs. Sanders, Carson is masturbating during class… frequently. Pretty much anytime he is sitting in his desk, he has his penis out of his pants."

"That surprises me," she said.

Her blue eyes opened wide. I could see where Carson got his adorable looks; his mother was sweet. The nurse mentioned her suggestion of laundry soap and larger underwear.

"Thank you for that note you all sent home." Mrs. Sanders nodded. "I can buy some things and try it this weekend. If that doesn't work, maybe you could just tell him to go to the bathroom to finish his business."

While I was relieved to get her cooperation, humping breaks at school just didn't seem right to me.

Principal Owen jumped in to the conversation then.

"Mrs. M., you'll need to document every time it happens."

I nodded my agreement, glad for the back-up.

"While it is not always the case, sometimes this behavior can indicate deeper issues or an incident of abuse," she continued. "We'll keep an eye on it for you, Mrs. Sanders, in case it warrants a call to Child Protective Services."

Later that week, Carson's mother took him to their pediatrician, who assured us via letter that the behavior was normal, though perhaps rather frequent.

In the weeks that followed the meeting, my antennae were focused on Carson. It was creepy to see him in the back of room, still red-faced and thumping, while I led reading groups with little first graders. Finally, I'd had enough.

"Carson, stop! You may do that at home. You may *not* do it in class."

And he stopped. Funny—all it took was a simple direction. I wished I'd been stern earlier. I noted the strategy in my profiles.

I asked around the school and every teacher reported one (or even two) Humpers in class. The nurse was so used to it that she did not immediately think of child abuse, but rather a child with poor social skills, little structure, or few rules at home.

If the behavior was combined with inappropriate drawings or sexual remarks, we teachers would compile a report to CPS. Mostly, we provided the child with limits and social awareness. Family used to be the place where children were socialized, but somehow the responsibility had shifted to the teacher.

I still felt that the majority of my job was to teach reading and math, and the behaviors were getting in the way.

****

The Recidivist: Adam would repeat first grade, hopefully not in my class. At seven, he was plenty old enough for second grade, but he was small and lacked the desire to be independent. I put 90 percent of my teaching effort into Adam and got about one percent academic improvement. His spelling tests were random letters scrawled across the page.

I referred Adam for an evaluation. All the observations and testing indicated no learning disabilities. He was just immature, and I recommended that he repeat first grade. His mother disagreed.

"I will not allow Adam to be retained. All you have to do, Mrs. M., is put him on your lap and you'd see he can read."

I was not about to put a seven-year-old boy on my lap. He was much too old for close physical contact from a non-family member, and I had 29 other students to teach.

I had an idea for a strategy and wrote it down in the profiles. This mother needed to see what second grade work looked like, and then she'd agree that Adam needed to be retained.

"Mrs. Bennett, I've gathered some sample materials from second grade so you can see the work that would be expected of Adam this fall. You can see that there are long paragraphs, with fewer pictures. We're setting him up to fail if he is passed to second grade."

"He can do all those on your lap," she insisted.

"But that would not be appropriate in a school setting," I told her. "And there are other things we consider in retention. Adam is small for his age, and his grades are low in all subjects. He still cries to go home for a good portion of the day. This is not what we expect in a successful second grader."

Mrs. Bennett withdrew Adam from Owen Charter and placed him in another school. Parents could do that in open enrollment districts when they were dissatisfied. I heard the new school also insisted that Adam repeat.

I looked into the future with my teacher's crystal ball. Adam would grow into a handsome man, go through several wives, each of whom would have the nurturing disease and want someone to "take care of." His mother would claim that the string of failed marriages and job losses were the fault of his first wife, "Emily," or that he'd always done just fine until he worked at the packing plant.

Until Adam learned what he needed to learn, and his mother learned to let him, he would keep repeating. There was nothing more I could do for him.

****

The Know-it-All: Jayla was sharp-eyed. She caught on quick to the first grade curriculum and would have preferred to teach the class herself. One day, she announced, "Mrs. M., my mother is going to homeschool me because I told her that you pronounced 'proboscis' incorrectly. She's not a teacher, but she knows more about teaching than you do."

I felt stripped naked in front of the class, as I fought my brain for an answer to this child. I pictured myself at her age, shy and on the bottom of the social food chain. I had never been as articulate as this Jayla kid, and probably still wasn't.

I tried hard to be everything that the kids, parents and school could want a teacher to be. If the child knew she was being pulled out for homeschooling, *it must be true*. It was probably meant as a direct insult to me.

But then again, if Jayla were gone, I wouldn't have to listen to her abrasive comments and that would make my life easier. She kept it up.

"Mrs. M., you already gave Sterling a turn at the chalkboard. When you were getting your teacher's training, didn't they require you to practice with actual children? You should have perfected giving turns by now."

I wrote down what the child said to me and showed it to Mrs. Gardener. She'd had Jayla's older brother and warned me to be careful when interacting with anyone in that family.

I needed a strategy for these confrontations, and it came straight from the animal world: I stood taller, bigger, and closer to frighten my challenger. I felt myself growing bolder from the posture alone, and I noted it in my files.

"Jayla, you are not the teacher in this class. I am. When you have your college degree, you come back and we'll talk."

"I'm going to let my mother know you spoke to me in that tone," she answered back.

"No, no. *I'm* going to let your mother know," I told her.

To get out of class, Jayla picked at her gums until they bled and then asked to go to the nurse. I decided to set a limit. I was the adult and she couldn't ruffle me anymore.

"Jayla, if you'd leave your mouth alone then you wouldn't bleed."

The next day I received a note.

As a teacher, you are not qualified to make medical decisions for my daughter. In the future, please speak to her with respect and defer all medical judgment to the school nurse or our family doctor.

Jayla smiled as I read the note. I could certainly see where she came by her attitude and articulate arguing. I was jealous.

I usually didn't like confrontation, but I didn't care about her insults anymore. They were still as shocking as she intended, but not at all true. I was the teacher, doing my job, and I had done the correct thing in trying to manage the child's behavior. It was the start of my teaching callous.

I was tempted to lash out at Jayla, to tell her how ugly I thought her attitude was, but I decided it was best to keep my interactions with this kid strictly professional and aloof. Then I documented every response by her mother. I added her to my profiles for future reference. There'd be more like her, and I'd worked too hard for my teaching certificate to have her kind of trouble.

****

The Chimney Sweep: Freckle-faced Arlene attracted a cloud of dirt. Her face and hands were brown with old grime. She wore shoes with no socks and smelled sweaty. Her clothes had the same dirt and jam smears for two days. She had a layer of grit on her desk and piles of sand under her feet. The other kids didn't seem to notice though, and she always had friends. Some kids were just grubbier than others, and it was never severe enough to warrant a call to Child Protective Services.

The weather turned warm, however, and the smells became unbearable: stale urine and sour skin. By the third day, the stench of *dirty butt* hung heavy in the air, so much so that Mrs. Gardener closed the adjoining door to my room. My urge was to avoid Arlene, but she needed help with her math facts. I offered her wipes to clean her face and arms.

I asked the school nurse to come visit the smells in my room. She called Arlene's mother to pick her up for an immediate shower. Her mother brought her back in five minutes. Arlene's hair had been combed, but she was wearing the same clothing and the rotting smell lingered.

I scheduled a conference with her mother and Principal Owen. I remembered my feelings of unpreparedness in the Humper's meeting, so I practiced this one ahead of time. Eventually, I settled on the speech.

"Mrs. Welch, I know that you bathe your children every night, but I think it might be time to supervise Arlene when she's soaping up. Kids like to splash around and jump out without getting a good scrub. I know she'd have a better experience at school with clean skin and clothes each day. If you need supplies, we can connect you with services."

After I'd said my piece at the meeting, I noticed Mrs. Welch had a layer of dirt around her neck, crusty elbows, and black gunk under her nails. Knowing Arlene, it didn't surprise me. I was fighting a losing battle.

Later, Principal Owen complimented me on conducting the delicate conversation in a non-offensive way. My tiny seed of confidence drank her words like water; I had skills, I was articulate—not like the obnoxious Know-It-All girl, but in a sensitive way, and I was proficient in a difficult part of the job. I wrote down the rehearsal strategy.

Arlene's family moved before the school year was over; her father had accepted a position as a pastor of a church. I wondered if the church had actually met them. It was sickening for poor Arlene to grow up like that, but being filthy was rather acceptable in our community. I hoped the church, if there really was one, would inspire them to clean up a little.

****

The Gifted Child Who *Wasn't*: On Meet the Teacher night, Cutter's father introduced himself to me.

"Cutter is a splendid reader. He's reading at a fourth grade level. Watch this. Sit in that chair, Cutter."

The father handed him a thick paperback book. Cutter held the book up to his face, pausing every so often to turn a page. I couldn't believe the father expected me to fall for this.

"Cutter, what is the title of this book?" I asked.

Cutter only shrugged.

"Who is it about?"

He shook his head and turned another page.

I turned to Cutter's father.

"Sir, we have standardized tests that will tell you Cutter's reading level."

"Mrs. M., my child is a genius. *I* am a genius. My wife's pretty smart too. You are not, so you wouldn't know what you are seeing here. Cutter doesn't need your tests. He needs to be put into the fourth grade."

"The fourth grade? He's six years old!"

I was torn between laughing and dreading this parent for the next year. Besides, why was this man's wife only "pretty smart," when the males in the family were geniuses?

I did some preliminary testing, and it turned out, Cutter was reading at an early first grade level, sounding words out. He was very teachable, and the father left me alone to do my job. I was glad because Cutter had a younger sister who was also pretty smart.

****

When I had several profiles put together, I began to wonder if teaching was worth it, if nearly every child was a landmine. Teaching was not what I'd expected, and a big part of me wanted to cut my losses and get out.

Mrs. Hill's words often played in my head.

You might never be a teacher.

But Mrs. Hill didn't have to beat me up. I had done that myself all those years after changing majors; I had not been living my first choice. Now I had the whole dream right in my lap. I couldn't throw it away again, even though I had a feeling the job had changed too much since I was child in the classroom. Possibly teaching had never been as much fun as it seemed.

I tried not to let it push my buttons. If I could get over the shyness and my fear of obnoxious personalities, it would be worth the thousands of dollars and years spent getting my certificate. It would be like free therapy.

I kept teaching with the purpose of seeing how many weird kids I could profile.

****

The Sleaze: Mallory was clearly not well-supervised when she got dressed each morning. She came to school wearing her teenage sister's red bra, fishnet stockings with a run, and elbow-length purple satin gloves. She put one hand in her armpit and pumped it quickly to make a fart sound. Other than that, her clothing included no pants, no shirt, no coat. I pointed her out to Mrs. Gardener, who sometimes kept extras for kids who needed to be covered up.

Even more disturbing than the clothing Mallory wore, which could be changed, was an attitude that couldn't. She lacked the innocence we tried to preserve in children. She made suggestions to other kids.

"Let's have sex at recess. Okay?"

I learned that *not* looking shocked was a big part of teaching, but Mallory needed more guidance than that. I tried to build character and social skills.

"Mallory, you have so many other things to talk about at school."

I discussed Mallory with the school nurse and Mrs. Gardener, with the child's mother, and with Principal Owen. We kept notes on Mallory's inappropriate clothing, provocative comments, behaviors, and the exact dates. Eventually, the school made a report to Child Protective Services, but nothing further came of it. It seemed that part of my job was simply to fill a parenting gap.

****

The Goat: Asher chewed everything, including his eraser, plastic scissors and books. The cuffs on his sleeves were soggy and shredded. Asher loved cheese puffs, and I could tell when he'd eaten them for lunch. His sleeves and the collar of his shirt would be bright orange and sopping wet.

I noticed Asher chewing on a white crayon one day.

"Asher, that's not good for you. Please take it out of your mouth."

He'd bitten off half of it, paper and all, chewed and swallowed it. I had a psych degree and had been a chalk eater myself, as a child. I knew that eating non-food items was a condition called pica, and I was a little concerned that Asher wouldn't stop. I called his mother, but she assured me Asher did this all the time at home. She wasn't worried.

One week when he had a cold, Asher ate all of his used Kleenex. I contacted his mother, who took him to the doctor. Recycled snot worried her.

"Mrs. M., if you don't mind, could you keep track of the number of Kleenex you give Asher? Sign them out to him and give him a smiley face when he places each one in the trash."

"I'll make a little chart for that. How many tissues can he have?"

"Well, he can have a new one in exchange for putting one into a trash that you monitor."

The job of teaching involved many tasks besides teaching. I was now juggling curriculum, behavior, and counting Kleenex on the side, but kids like the Goat kept me too busy to be self-conscious. I knew from last year's flooded teddy bear day that endless distractions were my friend, and I came to appreciate such tasks for their soothing qualities.

The thought occurred to me, *I'm not a teacher, but I play one on TV*. The acting implication somehow took away some of my social stress. I could teach because I was only pretending. If I acted competent, the kids believed I was. I repeated the line to myself several times a day and noted it in my strategy files. I also made a

supply of little charts for kid behaviors I'd need to track
and kept the master.

****

Student by Chance; Ignorant by Choice: Evan was
not interested in learning. His work was sloppy and he
was proud of that. His career plans included drinking
cheap beer and lying on the couch in an undershirt.
When I asked him to read his new spelling words, he
closed his eyes as if to ward off knowledge.

"I don't need to know this," he told me.

I visualized a normal fertilization, where a healthy
handsome sperm shows initiative by tracking down the
egg. The egg is busy getting some decorating ideas for
the nursery in *Family Circle*. The sperm pounces on her,
kisses her red lips, and together they work hard to create
a good, motivated student. Then I pictured another
sperm, off to the side, listlessly swimming in circles. A
different egg, clumsy and inattentive, trips over him.
That was how Evan got his start.

I mentioned my concerns to his mother, minus the
sperm story.

"Oh, I tell Evan not to worry about school," she
said. "He's already smart enough. Besides, no one ever
uses that stuff anyway."

I wanted to tell her that *I* do. I read, write and
balance my bank account. I converse appropriately.
Being able to function is not just a lifestyle. Even drug
dealers measure and make sales. I was angry at her for
implying my time and effort wasn't needed. With Evan
in mind, I reviewed my college textbooks on intelligence
theory and learning styles. Maybe I just hadn't found the
right way for Evan to enjoy school yet.

My plan was to get him to read enough so that he could have some choices later in life, so that he could read the label on his favorite beer someday. I noted my efforts in the strategy files, but Evan was difficult to motivate.

I questioned the direction our species was evolving. Many children seemed to value ignorance and laziness when an education was free. I wanted to yell at these kids.

"All right then! Just grow up dumb if you want to! Just grow up dumb!"

But I couldn't. I was supposed to *teach* them. It was my place to provide instructions for bettering their lots in life. I tried not to feel obsolete. There had to be students out there who wanted what I had to give.

****

The Bookworm: I appreciated students like Colleen. Colleen did not learn to read easily, but not because of a disability. She'd had so little exposure to books that she held them upside down as often as she held them correctly, or she flapped the covers and flew a book around the room. She pointed to the page in a book.

"Cats are fun. See? I'm reading!"

She wasn't.

I, myself, am at my happiest and most secure when I'm reading. It's one of the best cures for anxiety; a friend without the social tangles. Teaching kids to enjoy reading was a good fit for me. The focus was not on me, but on the book—pressure off. No matter how raw my nerves were, I was always willing to teach a student to read. For that, I had value in the teaching world.

I spent extra time with Colleen at recess. She was rich soil in the land of reading, and I had books to plant. We sat criss-cross applesauce—the politically correct term for "Indian style"—on carpet squares and turned to a page with simple three-letter words. The picture showed a boy, sitting in the kitchen.

"Colleen, let's look at the first word. Can you read what it says?"

"It says that guy is lazy and he won't go out and get a job!"

I thought of her home life. Her interpretation made perfect sense.

"No, he's a little boy. He doesn't need a job yet. But let's not guess about the picture. We're going to read what's on the page. Tell me the sound of the first letter."

"That's a B, and it says *buh*. The next one says *ih*."

"You're right. Do you know the last letter?"

"I don't know the ones with tails yet."

"You'll learn them." I smiled. Happy patience was required. "This is a letter G and in this word it says *guh*. Put these sounds together, and you can read."

She pointed to the word.

"B… i… g."

Her brow creased and her lips moved.

"BIG! That word says BIG!"

Our eyes locked, Colleen's and mine. It was a moment of complete understanding between our two minds on that day, in that room. It would take lots more practice, but the whole world would be hers for the choosing because of that moment I created for her.

The Bookworms were worth all the Screamers, all the difficult kids I'd profiled. Her type was worth every bit of time and energy I put into her. Forever, whether Colleen remembers me or not, I will be the teacher who showed her how to read. It happened many times every year, and it was the carrot that kept me going back to the classroom.

****

There were other profiles I learned to manage that second year of teaching: The Thief, The Wiggler, The Bully, The Gasless Car. A teacher friend suggested that I include a child she seemed to attract, "The Deliberate Vomiter." I was lucky never to have that one.

Who knows? Maybe as a child, I was some poor teacher's dreaded kid: *Oh no, not another Nervous Wreck!*

I was sure there were teachers and parents who would be horrified if they knew that I profiled, who would remind me that children were unique individuals, with beautiful gifts of their own, and that they could never be stereotyped. But those critics didn't live with my anxiety.

This secret profiling saved my sanity. Managing a large group became simpler. I knew what to expect from certain personalities, and I had a list of proven strategies to choose from. I had created a set of strengths and skills of my own that I didn't have to borrow from Mrs. Gardener.

I was able to divert my energy from coping with the tattering anxiety and out of control kids, to shaping their academic performance. Like the *Velveteen Rabbit*, I was real and had the missing patches of fur to show for it.

While I was at it, I decided to give my teacher profile a makeover. I'd always believed that a good teacher should be bubbly, passionate and "all about the kids." The romanticized version that I'd carried in my head since childhood had to go. I threw bubbly enthusiasm into the pile, along with the other things I wasn't going to worry about anymore. I stopped playing a teacher on television.

Being a good teacher required patience, not giddy energy. I could make the job mine—like the old Chinese proverb *teachers open the door to knowledge*. I didn't just open the door, I identified with it. Doors were not bubbly. Doors were dependable, solid, a clear path. That was my purpose.

I pictured myself meeting the next Screamer.

"Oh, hell! You're one of *those*? You just come right on in to my class, because I know what to do with you."

11
Start Each Song with a Spanking

"My mom would have spanked me," I told Mrs. Gardener.

I had finished compiling my first grader profiles and was trying to make sense of modern acceptable behavior.

"When I was a kid," I went on, "even *teachers* could spank you! Practically everybody could spank you. I once got spanked by another child!"

We were eating carrot sticks from my lunchbox in Mrs. Gardener's empty room.

"When I first started teaching," she said, "we could spank." A dreamy look came over her. "I'm sure that's what kept kids from getting as bad as they are now."

"*You* spanked your students?"

I could hardly imagine. Spanking was the physical act of striking another person on the backside, now considered a private part. It was a boundary I wouldn't dare to cross.

I recalled my own experience with being spanked; the sudden sting from out of nowhere, the uncertainty over what I'd done, my own hot tears. In the '70s, before parenting became popular, there was no discussion of choices, consequences, or even what I'd done to deserve it. Confusion and shame were part of the punishment.

Mrs. Gardener rolled her eyes.

"There were *guidelines*, of course. You couldn't lose your temper and the parents had to be called first. Then, you'd take the child to the office and give him one quick smack with the school paddle. It was wonderful. Word got around the playground and the whole class behaved well for a week, or even the rest of the year!"

I thought of my own elementary days.

I was a good girl, a good student. I would have died of pure humiliation if I'd been spanked at school. But there was usually one child who was unruly enough for a teacher to paddle in front of the group.

And teachers called students "bad." They weren't having a rough day, struggling or feeling bored. They were just *bad*, and spanking had a way of draining the bad out of the worst students. It was a huge deterrent for the rest of us.

Mr. Norton was my fifth grade teacher. He was a red-headed stocky man with rough-looking skin and Coke-bottle glasses. His temper matched his hair. As a warning, he'd thump kids hard on the top of the head with his knuckles.

"Boys! Let's play Monopoly!" he'd call out when he was happy.

The Monopoly table was presumably for reading groups, but Mr. Norton didn't write lesson plans, and reading groups were out that year. He and the boys, always just the boys, played marathon games. Occasionally, Cynthia and Kimberly were asked to cut and decorate additional paper money, adding it to Mr. Norton's stockpile.

He set up a couple of "learning centers" for the rest of us. A learning center in Mr. Norton's room was a two-pocket folder. If we were lucky, there was reading material in one pocket and a test in the other. If we were not lucky, the folder contained a blurry ditto, directing us to a dusty old textbook and a page of long division.

One day, the folder contained a vague, hand-scrawled assignment, due the following week. We were to make an art project about a book we liked.

I'd recently read a pioneer girl's story about her Indian friend. My mother helped me design a large doll from three pairs of pantyhose, a popular craft in the '70s. One pair of pantyhose, when stuffed, became the doll's legs, another pair the arms. The crotch of the third pair became the doll's forehead and scalp, and the stockings were cut and braided to form her hair. She was cute. My mom sewed a red velvet dress for her.

I took my doll to school, and nervously presented her to Mr. Norton and the class. Before I could even say the title of the book I'd read, Mr. Norton yelled.

"Pantyhose? I'm not even touching that!"

A warmth crept up my face and I could hear my pulse above the giggles of the class. He went on.

"I'm docking points on the pantyhose thing because her mom made its dress."

I wanted to defend my mother; she'd helped me make the doll. I loved her, but I was mad at her now, too. *How could she send me to Mr. Norton with pantyhose?*

Each morning after that, I dreaded the long walk to the lunchbox cubbies across the room. If Mr. Norton spotted me, he'd yell, "If it isn't Miss Pantyhose?"

My breath would catch in my throat as I pictured the doll's forehead, made from the crotch of the pantyhose.

Mr. Norton's moods confused me. My heart pounded as he flipped from marginally pleasant to red-faced and screaming. One day, he'd had it with us, all of us. We didn't even *try* to learn in his class, and he was *done*. His glasses fogged over with his yelling.

Vince, a curly-headed boy, was running around the classroom. This behavior had always been acceptable in

Mr. Norton's room before, and Vince wasn't the only one to do it.

Suddenly, Mr. Norton grabbed Vince by the arm and marched him to the front of the room.

"Lean over. Put your hands on the chalkboard."

Vince did.

Mr. Norton removed his own leather belt and smacked Vince on the behind with a loud thwack— three times.

"Now sit down!"

Vince wiped his eyes and walked to his desk where he put his head down.

The rest of us were stunned into quiet cooperativeness for a couple of days. Vince hadn't been *that* rowdy. Angry Mr. Norton was the real problem. I had a lot of stomach aches that year, and I stayed home from school as often as my mother would let me.

Despite Mr. Norton, I still wanted to be a teacher. If I were in charge, school would be safe and comfortable for everyone. Girls would play Monopoly too. I would not be at the mercy of someone who raged.

And yet I still was. Kids used to cope with ill-tempered teachers, and now teachers must cope with explosive kids. Teachers today have very few tools available for even seriously disruptive children, and certainly not spanking.

My Screamer, Monica, had been on a silly consequence program. I had to show her a "thumbs up" for cooperating or a "thumbs down" for screaming. If I myself were in a screaming rage, I don't think I'd care about the direction of someone's thumb. I wondered what one of Mr. Norton's spankings might have done for Monica or for Tyson.

There were several class management systems endorsed by schools where teacher friends of mine worked. "Pulling a Card" was a pocket-chart of colored squares, beginning with green for positive behavior.

When a child pulled so many warning cards from the chart that they came to a red one, the parents were called. Some teachers took recess minutes away, but this often backfired, because kids' rowdy energy wasn't burned off.

Owen Charter posted a happy face and a sad face on the chalkboards. We teachers wrote student names underneath to describe behavior. This resulted in the gain or loss of a daily sticker. It was a risky method though. The instructors in teachers' college warned us that teachers and schools had been sued for writing names on the chalkboard. It was considered public humiliation.

We never called it punishment at Owen Charter. The students simply earned consequences for behavior. More often, I was punished by the parents for giving consequences. I found myself trying to balance between managing kids' behavior and knowing parents would be in after school to argue with me about it.

"Mrs. M., I got your note. Do you really think that Garrison needs to be on the sad face for talking out? Your poorly thought out seating arrangement is to blame for his distraction, not Garrison."

I listened, but I did not remove consequences.

Just for fun, I did an Internet search and found that many states banned corporal punishment. Arizona is not one of them, but I never heard of a child being spanked in school in my years of teaching, either at preschool or Owen Charter.

During a chaotic musical rehearsal at Owen, kids were jumping around the stage, throwing straw hats at each other and pulling on the curtains. Everyone was screaming a different song and refusing to settle in for practice.

The frustrated music director hissed, "This performance would be so much better if we could just start each song with a *spanking!*"

I pictured a subdued group of cooperative children, hands folded in front of them, teary and quietly waiting for instruction—their shifty-eyed looks replaced with humble innocence. She was right about spanking, but teachers would probably have served jail time.

12
Nature's Way

Mrs. Gardener, and I followed Owen Charter's first grade curriculum together. We took turns doing the weekly first grade shopping for art supplies. We called each other on the weekends to discuss who had the wackier students. I looked forward to my days with Mrs. Gardener. She was the handlebars on my bicycle of teaching.

Each spring, we taught a long unit on the life cycle of butterflies. Although I was eager to do any project with Mrs. Gardener, I'd had a bad experience with butterflies.

When I was four years old, my mother wanted to show me the beautiful miracle. She found two cocoons hanging outside under our kitchen window and put them in a clean Gerber's baby food jar. With a hammer and nail, she punched air holes in the lid. My mother was powerful and knew so much about everything.

The next morning, we were able to watch one hatch before breakfast. We admired the butterfly's brave struggle to escape his gray cocoon. My mother opened the jar and gently shook him onto the back porch so he'd have room to do his work. He slowly fanned his gooey wings until they became silky and black with orange spots. Then he flew away to begin his butterfly life.

"See?" my mother said. "It's a miracle."

The other one hatched while we were gone to church. When we returned that afternoon, we checked the jar and found the beautiful butterfly crunched and miserable. The jar was too small for his wings to dry properly.

"This one won't make it," she told me. "He needs to go to heaven where he won't hurt anymore. You wait in the house."

I followed her outside. I wanted to see how she would help the butterfly get to heaven. Maybe I'd want to go too. What I saw was my mother, the source of all strength and knowledge, using a yard stick to mash the butterfly's head off.

"Get back in the house!" she yelled at me.

But I had already seen her way of helping things get to heaven and I no longer wanted to go. I'd often remind her of this when she hugged me with those same arms.

"You're not going to squish me up to heaven, are you?"

And now, I taught at Owen Charter, where the butterfly life cycle was a huge part of the science curriculum. Every spring, Mrs. Gardener ordered two kits through the mail. Each kit contained a large mesh hutch, a poster, and a cup of six tiny caterpillars with a brown sugar-like substance caking the bottom. As they became fat, hairy caterpillars, the plastic cup filled with their poop.

They'd cocoon, and at least one of *mine* would drop to the bottom dead, leaving me with a lot of bug-touching and explaining to do. During my first year of teaching, I had Mrs. Gardener secretly remove the dead one for me. Later, I explained to the class.

"No, I think we only had *five*…"

In my second year, I was more direct.

"Sometimes, like Emily's grandma, caterpillars *die*."

Then I put on plastic gloves and transferred the remaining cocoons into their hutch. Mrs. Gardener and I held an ongoing competition between our classes to see whose butterflies would hatch first and "win."

Each morning, we'd open our adjoining door and parade our hutches through both classes to show off our caterpillars' growth. The students would groan and cheer. Even things I wouldn't enjoy on my own took on an element of fun with Mrs. Gardener.

That year, the butterfly kits arrived too early in the season. Our classes did all the journaling and the observing of caterpillars before spring break. As the last child was loaded into his car for the week off from school, the first butterfly hatched.

Mrs. Gardener and I sat in silence, officially on vacation, patiently watching her newborn butterfly dry its wings.

"I'm leaving for Ohio," she said.

"Yeah."

"I know butterflies are kind of creepy for you."

Butterflies in a hutch required daily care. They needed fresh sugar water and an orange slice. They needed someone to tell them how pretty they were, even though they looked like old gray moths.

"I'm a big girl." I shrugged. "I can take both hutches home for the week. Maybe they'll last until the kids come back to school."

By that night, all six of Mrs. Gardener's butterflies hatched out, big and healthy. She always won the competition—even when she wasn't there to compete.

One of my cocoons had already fallen into the poop and died days earlier. I woke up the first morning of spring break and four of my butterflies had hatched, small but alive. The last one was still struggling to break free from a cocoon as tight and pinchy as Sunday shoes. Without the audience of 30 children, my courage and the miracle of the butterfly disappeared. I called my mother and asked if she remembered anything about butterfly heaven.

"Well…I know you don't like killing things, but there's always the toilet. It would be for the best."

I curled my lip and reached into a hutch to change the sugar water. The last butterfly was still thrashing, stuck in her paper prison. Maybe she'd do better if I wasn't looking. I ate breakfast, took a shower, checked my email… and still no butterfly.

Finally, one crunched wing emerged. I felt somehow at fault for not doing something sooner. I pictured my mother and her murderous yardstick. If my husband had been home, I would have made him do something. But, this was clearly a butterfly emergency that I'd have to take care of by my brave adult self.

I gently put the cocoon on a paper towel on my kitchen table. The poor thing was flopping hard and looked exhausted. I couldn't stand it anymore. Maybe that's how my mother felt all those years before, as her little girl looked on, waiting for a miracle. Now it was my job and, even without my class, I was still the teacher.

I got my husband's mustache scissors, took a deep breath, and cut the crackly cocoon away from the butterfly. She lay still and relieved. I placed a fresh orange slice under her tongue. In the long struggle to hatch, her wing and head had dried crumpled.

She lay near the orange slice, drinking in the cool juice. Her black eyes looked glad to be alive and not ready to be mashed up to heaven. I watched over her that day and made sure she was comfortable. I felt a little silly to be scared of her; she was only grateful and meant me no harm. That evening, my butterfly found her own way to heaven. I didn't have to send her with a flush or the yardstick.

Over spring break, I got to looking at Mrs. Gardener's butterflies, big and healthy with no effort at all. I called her in Ohio.

"Your butterflies are awfully mature," I reported.

"Of *course* they are. It's because I'm such a good teacher," she laughed.

"Yeah, but wait until you see what they're doing."

Her butterflies had clearly reached adulthood, confident in their right-sized skin. They even enjoyed sexual relations, involving a long red appendage and lots of excited flapping. Mrs. Gardener's butterfly boys were not picky either. They finished with one girl and moved right on to the next, without so much as a "See you around the sugar water, babe."

"I'll have a talk with them when I get back."

When spring break ended and I brought the butterflies back to school, Mrs. Gardener's bunch was still at it.

"Good luck explaining *that* to your class," I told her as I handed her the hutch. I pictured the kids asking, "Teacher, what is that long red thing?"

My butterflies were pensive loners, quietly reading books in their own corners. There was no dance party in my hutch. For once, I thought, I had the easier lesson in teaching, with no awkward explaining to do.

After our tear-filled ceremony for releasing the butterflies back to nature, school ended for the day and I tracked down Mrs. Gardener.

"What did you tell the kids?" I asked, savoring her turn at nervous squirming.

"I just said that this is nature's way."

I laughed out loud. Like her butterflies, Mrs. Gardener was comfortable in a way I would never be. I envied her. Even her street address had a happy-go-lucky name, while mine included the word *Desperado*.

After I'd seen the butterfly cycle a couple of times, I began to compare that miracle with students learning to read—or not. As much as parents wanted a tiny first grade caterpillar to fly like a big second grade butterfly, she couldn't until she grew her wings. They could even put her in the hutch with the butterflies and say, "She flies just fine at home." But the caterpillar couldn't fly until she grew her wings.

Reading was like that.

Teaching was like that, for me.

When I mentioned this theory to Mrs. Gardener, she said, "You'd be happier if you didn't put quite so much thought into things."

"Yeah. It's just nature's way."

13
Sketchy Conception Stories

If I was honest with myself, I'd gone into teaching partly because I was more comfortable around children. Adults were able to insult me, threaten me, or get me fired. Then I realized that students came with parents attached.

The worst were overachieving parents, who bought commercial reading programs like *Your Baby Can Read!* They were nearly as uptight as I was, and they expected me to *Prepare Their First Grader for College!* The best thing to do, for them and for myself, was to recite a prepared and assertive response on how I would challenge their child. Then I met Mr. Peterson.

When he was raising his first family back in the early '70s, he was disinterested, the way fathers were supposed to be. Now quite elderly and retired, he'd married a much younger and possibly mail-order bride. Together, they had William, and Mr. Peterson focused all his remaining energy on the boy.

For his parent conference, he brought William's report card and a stack of assignments he'd been saving.

"Mrs. M., I want you to prove, based on this work, that William has a 95 percent, and not a 96 or a 97 percent."

My old fear of adults kicked in with a vengeance, but I vowed to stop feeling like the inferior omega dog, exposing my soft underbelly. I was an experienced professional and didn't need to back down anymore.

"William's grades are based on test scores," I told him. "Not all of the assignments you have there went in the grade book."

Mr. Peterson wrote down the scores I read to him and double checked my math on scratch paper.

"Okay, then where does William rank among the other students? Top ten? Top five?" he asked.

"Sir, we don't figure rank at Owen Charter. William has an A average."

"Well, estimate. Top five? Top three?"

I shrugged.

"I'd have to say top five. He's a strong student."

I felt badgered, until I began to see beyond this man's withered face. He was stressed and anxious, like me, underneath his pushy talk. It seemed he clung to William as if he were losing his foothold by an open grave.

"He'll get the stick until he's at the top one percent," the man said. "We keep an old paint stirrer hanging on the wall for William's paddlings. I may need to knock some teachers' heads together while I am it."

I used a trick they taught us in teachers' college and pressed my tongue against the back of my teeth to keep from cursing. I'd been too shy to need it before. A good sign though: anger beat fear.

His wife sat next to him, a silent Thai woman with waist-length hair. To change the subject, I complimented her.

"I love your hair, Mrs. Peterson. It's beautiful."

She smiled, while Mr. Peterson glared at me.

"You could be attractive too," he said, "if you'd try. That's what's wrong with American women. That's why I didn't marry *you*."

I laughed. That wasn't the *only* reason he didn't marry me. I wondered what conditions his wife had suffered in her homeland to make this man an improvement.

The family was moving anyway, Mr. Peterson explained, so William could go to a decent school. I was happy for them, and very happy for me. Despite Mr. Peterson's snarling, I had put my shoulders back and stepped forward. I hadn't even needed my prepared response.

****

Medically diagnosed allergies were fairly common in a large class, usually involving peanuts, dairy products, or gluten. I stayed in close contact with the parents of those children to ensure safety. But Aubrey's mother, Mrs. Hicks, was a little extreme. She was so devoted to Aubrey and her allergies that she was virtually Munchausen in her parenting style.

"Aubrey is *allergic!*" Mrs. Hicks emphasized each syllable. "She is allergic to the regular yellow pencils and needs to use the black-painted pencils. They're impossible to find locally. I drive into the city at least twice a week for her brother's breathing treatments, and I can get you more pencils then if you let me know 24 hours ahead of time."

"An allergy to yellow pencils?" I asked. "That's unusual. Thanks for letting me know."

"Also, Aubrey cannot use aloe or even non-aloe baby wipes, and certainly not bleach wipes to clean her desk, so I brought a package of natural sea sponges for you to moisten and dispose of."

I was starting to get the picture. The child was likely fine, but her mother was a wreck. It felt good to know that I wasn't the only adult struggling to cope with anxiety. I could smell it on this woman. Apparently, she didn't know that while I used to play a teacher on television, I now played a psychiatrist and enjoyed diagnosing her issues instead of mine.

"And, really important," Mrs. Hicks went on. "Aubrey isn't allowed to sit next to other children who use brand name crayons. She's highly allergic to the dye in the wax. I'd really prefer that the whole class go dye-free out of concern for Aubrey's well-being."

I doubted that would ever happen.

"What kind of symptoms should I look for?" I asked her.

"Oh, you don't want to know. Also, she can't eat anything that contains salad oil, rye, or any type of seaweed derivative."

"I really do need to know what type of symptoms to watch for, just in case she has a reaction."

Other parents were waiting to "Meet the Teacher," so I tried to finish.

"Can you please write all this information down for me? I'll give a copy to the school nurse. If you have doctor's notes for us to keep on file, that's even better."

"I've tried for years to get the doctor to document her symptoms. I do a lot of research online and I know she has some kind of syndrome. Her brother is the same way. It's a weakness in our genes. Just be careful with her, okay? And call me for any little thing. I will always come get her. Lots of times, an extra bath in special soap is what she needs when she's been exposed to some of these toxins."

As the school year went on, Mrs. Hicks would often sit in the back of my room, worried that Aubrey might be "coming down with something." Every few minutes, she'd run up and place her wrist on Aubrey's forehead to check for fever. Eventually, she'd get tired of waiting for Aubrey to exhibit symptoms and take her home for some organic chicken broth, "just in case."

She never harmed Aubrey, and I did not hold the over-protective behavior against her. My own nerves just happened to manifest themselves differently. By checking, checking, and checking on her child, she was reassuring herself of her own necessity and devotion. She was soothing her own nerves, much like I used to when I sat on the floor of my closet, protecting myself from the world and regrowing emotional skin.

I gave Mrs. Hicks my respect, patiently reminding her that Aubrey was safe in my classroom, and I provided her daughter with a good education.

****

Not all parents were overachievers. My favorites had sketchy conception stories and made whimsical life decisions. I thought back to my mental health work days in the clinic.

I myself had returned to teaching on the advice of a prostitute on my caseload, and he had given me good guidance. Somehow, he had recognized a weakness— and a strength—in me that I hadn't yet been willing to address. I was no one to judge.

Like me, these parents had every reason to be worried about life. But apparently they weren't. I wondered why I was. I studied them.

Whimsical parents had breezy ways of organizing their lives, unbothered by social norms. Their thoughts seemed comfortable. Interacting with them gave me a taste of confidence, and I liked it.

Miss Dalton came to Owen Charter to pick up her children, wearing a longish T-shirt and nothing else. She lived with her children's father and dated other men openly. She might bring a skinny tattooed man with her one week, and a heavy-set cowboy the next. The father of the kids mentioned these other men to me, but he didn't seem to mind. I would have had a breakdown in his place.

One sunny day, I noticed two people sitting "spider style"—one straddling the other—on a playground swing. I assumed it was a couple of middle school kids and went over to remind them of the rules—spider style was not allowed at Owen Charter because of the close contact. But, it was Miss Dalton and her new boyfriend.

I mentally ran through some things a responsible teacher might say: "Move along, lovebirds," or "If the students can't do it, neither can you." I briefly considered, "Can I have a turn?"

However, these people were minding their own business. I had no reason to assert myself, so my best solution was to stand at the office window and stare until another staff member went outside and took care of it.

I was not proud of that, though. I liked this family, and they were friendly. I made it a goal to do better. I was calmer now on the inside, so I could be more direct on the outside. I deserved to be assertive.

****

Ms. Price, a wiry truck driver, visited my classroom to help with her son's reading group. We used *Red Riding Hood*, a small picture book with beginner words on each page. After listening to her group read, Ms. Price pulled me aside, her eyes wide.

"Mrs. M., there is explicit content in this book!" she whispered.

"In *Red Riding Hood*?" I'd read the book a hundred times. It was traditional and simple. "I guess I don't understand what you mean, Ms. Price."

"There are words in this book that are sexual," she nodded for emphasis.

I'd never had a parent look me in the eye and say such a thing. As I had promised myself, I was practicing my assertive tone and eager to be direct in this rather silly situation. If nothing else, I'd have a good story to tell my teaching buddy, Mrs. Gardener.

I looked around, cautious of children who might be listening.

"Could you be specific?"

Ms. Price flipped some pages and pointed to a sentence.

"Right here. Red Riding Hood *came* to Grandma's house. That's offensive in a children's book. Red Riding Hood enjoyed a sexual encounter."

"A sexual encounter with *who*?" I asked. The only options in this version were, heaven forbid, Grandma, or even worse, the wolf.

"It doesn't *matter* who!" she gasped, shaking her head.

"Thank you for this information." I smiled. "I'll let Principal Owen know."

And I did let her know, immediately. I thought of Ms. Price, rather hard and workaday. It probably took more guts for her to approach a teacher than it did for me to respond. But she couldn't be allowed to volunteer with children anymore.

"Why do you get all the weird ones?" Mrs. Gardener asked.

"It's an energy thing," I told her. "It'll stop when I learn to be confrontational."

****

Some parents look up their child's teacher on the Internet, and many teachers have websites and blogs that cater to interested parents. Most parents probably didn't realize that I Googled them too. I could do it safely from home and find out all kinds of things, without having to actually talk to anyone. It was a win-win, for me anyway.

My student, Tagan, cursed a lot and hardly ever had lunch or weather-appropriate clothing. That was plenty of reason for concern, so one night, at home, I typed his mother's name into a search engine.

Tagan's mother had a website referring to herself as a "Rug Devil." She described her wooly, love-rug that could be moved from room to room to mark a special site.

"Nothing says Valentines' Day like a blow job!" she proclaimed on her website.

She included nearly-nude photos of herself and daily updates on the positions she and her husband were trying in order to conceive another child.

"A gift in my belly" she called it.

I hoped the gift in her belly would be better behaved than its brother. It did explain Tagan's colorful vocabulary.

When I met with Tagan's parents for a conference, I kept picturing the love-rug, now matted and stained, and tossed in a corner of the kitchen. Suddenly, I had nothing to be afraid of. These were very casual people who came to school because their child's teacher asked them to.

I mentioned Tagan's lack of a jacket and lunch and was impressed when they apologized and thanked me. Tagan usually had what he needed after that. Apparently, an older sibling had been driving him to school and hadn't checked for necessities. The parents could keep their love-rug.

****

A quirky home life is certainly not unique to today's culture. When I was a first grader back in the '70s, a stubby red-headed boy from school asked me to walk home with him. His name was Eric. I'd known him since kindergarten so I expected his parents to be similar to mine: older, clean, and bent on divorcing each other.

Eric told me there were collie puppies at his house. I wanted to play with a puppy and possibly take a cute one home. Puppy stories now evoke a hint of being lured into molestation, but this was innocent. Eric had been telling the truth. He did have puppies. Swarms of them!

Eric's mother was, by today's definition, an animal hoarder, although she probably would have preferred the term "breeder." They had not just one litter of collies, but many.

Adult dogs ran freely through the house and did their business where they pleased. The carpet was barely visible through the layers of fur and stepped-on piles of dog poop. The air burned with the smell of urine. Box after cardboard box contained yipping pups. Kennels of more barking dogs lined the back porch.

Eric's mother smiled and invited me in. She was as red-headed as Eric was, wore a flowered house dress, and she was very sweet to me, but I could hardly believe what I was seeing.

Since I liked dogs much more than I liked people, I was not at all afraid. I just hadn't known that there were adults in the world, nice ones, who let things get so dirty and out of control. Where were the good decisions, the tidy kitchen, the cookie smell that was supposed to go with a mother? This woman confused me. I didn't know what to do with friendly filth.

Looking back, I wonder if she was coping with an anxiety too, and had surrounded herself with the comfort of animals. As an adult, I certainly prefer her kind of friendly filth over smiling, mean people. Those are the ones who can do some damage.

I described Eric's puppies to my own mom when I got home, hoping that she'd let me keep one, but she didn't. We already had a dog, and my mom liked our house orderly. I was rather relieved that I wouldn't have to go back to Eric's hairy house, even for a puppy.

After that, I took more notice of my friends' parents. The girl next door had a grouch for a dad. The parents across the street whispered and wore beads around their necks. Another mother had bright red lips and could remove any splinter with her hard fingernail. My own parents seemed about as weird as everyone else's, but mine were a comfortable and familiar weird.

****

At Owen Charter, stay-at-home dads were becoming more common. Mr. Linnert was such a dad. His work was to lecture us teachers on the dangers of the sun. It seemed reasonable at first, as everyone knew about sunburn and skin cancer. But then he began to elaborate.

Inside the sun, Mr. Linnert claimed, were alien beings, and if a human stood in the sun without the head covered by tin, the aliens would eat the brain. He began fashioning tin foil hats for all the teachers. His two children also wore them.

I politely declined.

One day, Mr. Linnert decided that I wasn't teaching correctly.

"The aliens have gotten to your brain," he explained. "You're wasting the children's time with inactive learning, like recess."

"My brain is fine," I assured him, and it *was*, pretty much. Better than it used to be anyway.

But he placed a reclining lawn chair in the back of my classroom, along with a gallon jug of water and a spiral notebook. He lay there, pencil poised to take notes, observing, as parents were allowed to do.

I waited for his scrutiny to chase away my effectiveness as a teacher, giving him something negative and critical to write down. But Mr. Linnert was a self-contained capsule of oddity.

I've come to sense that about certain people. They are so caught up in their own thoughts that they're not intimidating. I brought out my friendly voice.

"Mr. Linnert, would you like to help?" The students were painting, and the extra hands would be welcome. But apparently he didn't enjoy the pleasant chatter and the high energy in the room.

"Nah," he said. "I'm going home."

And off he went, wearing his tin foil hat. His departure was his approval. I had the class under control, so there was nothing for him to note.

I stood a little taller.

****

As my confidence grew, so did my gut feelings and my willingness to listen to them. Mrs. Bartell wrote important notes to me, in pencil, between the sentences of her daughter's book reports. I didn't get the mother's notes until I graded at night.

One of little Stacy's assignments went like this:

"I like cats. Cats are small animals with soft fur. *Mrs. M., Stacy will be absent tomorrow for a dental appointment. Please send her missed work home today. Thanks, Mrs. Bartell.* They have kittens and feed them milk. I wish I had a kitten at home and that's why I liked this book."

It seemed strange of her, but I was willing to let people have their differences.

But then Mrs. Bartell complained to Principal Owen that some of us teachers were evil and were injuring her children. No injuries were found on the children, but Mrs. Bartell claimed we were so evil that the bloody wounds had healed instantly.

This was something we teachers would not tolerate. Differences in communication were one thing, but false accusations were another. We started saving Mrs. Bartell's notes and documenting phone conversations.

One afternoon, I was getting my class ready for dismissal. Stacy stood out of line and looked like she had something wet on her mouth. I almost let it go; we were late, and it was the end of the day. But my gut told me to take the time and investigate.

"Stacy, there is something on your face."

She just stood there, not speaking.

"Stacy, are you blowing spit bubbles? There is something shiny on your mouth."

She didn't respond.

I walked up to Stacy and saw it: clear packing tape. She had removed the tape from her name tag and put it across her own mouth. I certainly would *never* do that to her or any child. I was calm and discreet.

"Stacy, take the tape off. We don't do that."

I watched while she removed the tape. It left no marks or chapped lips. It had been stuck to her desk too long to be very sticky. I immediately called Principal Owen and discussed the incident report I would write.

I was proud of my teacher self. I had grown an inner voice. I wasn't sure if it was new, or if I was now willing to listen to it. Either way, I could only imagine the consequences, the end of my career, if I'd allowed Stacy to get into her mother's car with tape over her mouth. I was grateful not to be writing books from the prison for convicted teachers.

Owen Charter recommended that teachers carry a two-million dollar teacher liability policy. We paid the premiums ourselves. Now, whenever the national news reports a "taped mouth" in a classroom, I think there must be more to the story than a teacher gone crazy.

****

I thought Mrs. Perez might be another hovering critic, as she spent so much time at Owen Charter. I spoke to her first, marking my territory as a competent teacher. She gave me a warm hello in her soft accent.

"For years, I wanted to teach, but God had other plans."

A gifted cook, Mrs. Perez prepared fresh, homemade tortillas with egg filling. She brought her burritos every day in a crock pot to keep them hot. I watched her offer teachers, different teachers each day, an egg burrito.

"Did you eat? You cannot work empty."

Somehow, she always knew which teachers needed her food. *A free spirit,* I thought, *one of those whimsical parents that I liked so much.*

One Monday before school, Mrs. Perez sensed I was having a migraine. I got them often when a quiet, recuperative weekend ended with the morning roar of the classroom. She came to my desk, patted my hair.

"You have a sick headache?"

I wiped my eyes.

"I don't think I can teach kids today."

She gave me an egg burrito.

"Eat this. I will pray for you. Go slow. You will feel better."

Already feeling off balance, I sat crying and eating the burrito. Soon, my headache was better. Completely better—no migraine, no tears, no hiding. With admiration, I took Mrs. Perez out of the categories. She was above that.

While a few parents would always be out to challenge me, to question my competence and make me flex my fear muscles, I could trust the whimsical parents not to criticize me. I could enjoy the conversations I had with them.

Chronic social worry was my own approach to life, but I was learning to stand up to it. My brain was getting healthier and controlling my nerves, instead of the other way around.

After Mrs. Perez, I wondered how many truly good people I had missed out on because of the anxious storm inside.

14
The Things We Bring to School

I carried a pocketful of medicine to school as a child—vitamin C tablets, when I was fighting a cold and an aspirin for my headaches, with my mother's strict instructions to "eat" it after lunch.

I especially liked her potassium medication; orange-tasting, fizzy tablets, that dissolved in water like a small soda. I took a couple of those, so I'd have something fun to add to my drink at lunch. Lots of times, I ended up sucking on the tablets in class and wiping the orange foam on my sleeve.

Owen Charter, however, had strict, nurse-administered medicine policies. One day, Mrs. Gardener and I scheduled both of our classes to watch a video on penguins for the science unit. As we made room on the floor for group seating, a large, amber prescription bottle rattled out of Kylie's desk. It was full of pills in a variety of sizes and colors, and the pharmacy label named an older boy at Owen Charter. Odd...

The nurse talked to Kylie, whose response was innocent.

"I have a sore throat, and my mom would want me to take medicine."

After an immediate phone call, Kylie's parents rushed her to the ER. Mrs. Gardener and I heard later that they had her stomach pumped. She stayed home for a couple days, but she was fine. We were relieved that Kylie hadn't suffered any ill-effects and that her parents didn't sue the school.

Apparently, the boy who dropped the pills had visitation with a non-custodial parent, and the bottle contained a week's supply of his prescriptions. He'd forgotten to leave it with the nurse, and it had fallen from his duffle bag on the playground.

Kids brought other things to school, as well. Cell phones with their loud ring tones and dance music were to be signed into the office before school, but even the youngest students at Owen Charter managed to hide them. I found one buried in the sandbox, and the wallpaper picture was of a six-year-old girl in my class. When I contacted her mother, she was straight-forward.

"We want her to have her own phone. Just in case."

"In case of what?" I asked.

"Well, so she can tell me if she has no one to play with at recess, or if she doesn't like her tuna sandwich, you know. Or, there might be a crazed shooter in the school."

I'd thought that's what she was getting at— everyone's horror. Still, I didn't appreciate the reminder that teaching could be tragic, that I had more to fear. The daily tasks were enough to keep me overwhelmed.

"You know," I told Mrs. Gardener one day at lunch, "When I was a kid, a lot of the boys carried pocket knives and gouged things on the playground."

"I remember those days. I guess weapons policies hadn't been invented yet."

Owen Charter, like every school in America, had an explicit policy that students did not bring toys, weapons or any other non-lunchbox or homework-related items to class. As a teacher, I understood this was a safety precaution, but the students took it as a dare.

Ben, a first grader of mine, dug through his backpack one afternoon.

"Hey!" he yelled. "Look at this!"

"That's cool!" someone called out.

"Mrs. M.—Ben has a *gun*!"

I held my breath.

"Ben has a *what*?"

And there it was, a shiny black gun, lying across his open palms. There was no tell-tale orange paint on the barrel that would mark it as a toy.

I looked into the child's large, green eyes. The situation felt enormous. This six-year-old's decision could kill me or children in my care. *I should be scared!* I thought to myself. The world around me seemed to swirl and fall apart, but strangely, I did not panic.

The ever-present prickle of nerves quieted. It seemed that one of two things had to be a mess—me, or the rest of the world. When Ben brought the gun out, I stepped out of my fear, like an old wet towel, and became comfortable, functional. I didn't seek disaster, but I did savor that moment of inner calm.

"Ben, put it on my desk, okay?" I nodded encouragement.

By my second year of teaching, I'd learned that kids often did what I told them to do. I waited. A shoe scraped the grit under a chair. A pencil tapped. Ben blinked.

"Okay, Mrs. M., but isn't it an awesome gun? It's my dad's."

"Mm hmm. Recess!"

I ushered the whole class out to the playground with an aide and called administration.

"One of the kids just put a gun on my desk."

Only then did my heart begin to pound. I pictured blood that could have pooled on the floor, children that could have been silenced in death—things that have come so quickly to other schools.

There were steps that administrators were required to take: the police were called, the building evacuated for further searching, and parents informed.

Mrs. Gardener stood next to me in our assigned evacuation places on the playground. She squeezed my hand.

"Hey, you did a good job."

"Thanks," I nodded. "This whole thing scared the crap out of me!"

"Of course it did. It would me, too, and I've been teaching forever."

Ben's gun turned out to be a toy from his dad's childhood collection, years before the orange paint regulation. I'd done the right thing, they told me in the office. Schools today have the "zero-tolerance" policy on weapons, even toy ones.

It seems incredible when adults compare it to our own supervision-free childhoods, but in our current social climate, the line has to be drawn at safety.

Ben was suspended for the day, in-school. He had to write apologies to the class and to me. Our Fire Pal, a local firefighter in charge of educating school children about 911 and fire prevention, gave a talk on gun safety.

A deep certainty grew in the panic center of my brain. If I could handle all those kids I'd profiled, their parents, and now kids with guns and do it calmly and do it right, then this teaching job wasn't bigger than me.

I still felt the low-burning sizzle under my skin some mornings as I greeted my students. But now a bit of confidence rested inside me, and I was starting to feel like I deserved to be a teacher.

After the gun incident, I began to pay closer attention to the menagerie of things kids brought to school. For my birthday, a boy in my class brought me a zipped sandwich bag, full of water, and in it, a green plastic alien.

"This is for you, Mrs. M. It's from my mom."

Yes, that's just the kind of gift I would expect from one woman to another. I smiled, displayed the bag on my desk for the day, and admired it often.

After school, I poured the water out but kept the alien, a reminder of the breathing child who'd given it to me.

15
How Much Ya Got?

I woke up, sniffling with a headache and sore throat. If I'd had any other job, I certainly would have stayed home in pajamas, sipping hot sweet tea, with lemon. I lay in bed, debating briefly. This was the last day of school. A substitute couldn't say goodbye to my students for me.

Suddenly I knew. This group of first graders *needed* me—*plain old me*. I could do for them what no other teacher could, because of who they were and who I was, and how we worked together.

I drove to school and braced myself for the ways of any last thing. No matter how many times I'd wished for the year to end, the last day felt so abrupt. The kids left, some of them forever.

The world I'd created in my classroom was no more. Everything that seemed so crucial, that caused me frustration and joy, was finished. Endings brought out my separation anxiety.

Because the change was so sharp, I offered my students the type of comfort that had helped me: My favorite old *Timmy Mouse* book from when I was a child.

I'd owned a copy of the Miriam Clark story back then, but when my parents split up, there was an unfortunate yard sale, and someone bought the book for a dime. I was heartbroken and never forgot Timmy and his sister mouse, who lost their parents, which I could relate to in a divorce sort of way.

The mice eventually found each other, and everyone went happily back to their mouse house. That ending didn't happen for me. My parents stayed apart, and my own big brother grew up and moved away. Unfortunately, I didn't remember the title correctly and ended up buying every 1960's mouse-related book on eBay.

Earlier, that second year of teaching, my mother was diagnosed with bone cancer. No one was sure if she'd pull through. The thought of being without her was unbreathable and searing.

Somehow, I managed to cope with both the worry over my mother and my nerves in the classroom. I went back to the things that had helped me when Dr. Ford stopped prescribing medication. I went to bed earlier.

When I could make the time and force myself to relax, I soaked in the silent balm of sleep that made cancer and school and everything else disappear. I treated myself to comforting, stable things like plain vanilla ice cream or an old brown sweater. There was so much anxiety swirling around me that food and clothing didn't need to be exciting.

Walking a couple miles after school each day took the blistering edge off, footsteps in front of more footsteps. I walked myself *away* from the possibility of her dying. These things kept the stresses from combining to make me faint, or vomit.

I'd always done better in the classroom with other distractions going on anyway. So rather than overwhelming me, the classroom became my most predictable place. I probably couldn't have absorbed much more, though. One critical observer or a poor evaluation on top of my mom's illness, and I would have panicked.

Her doctor scheduled some final tests before chemotherapy. The results were crucial. I took the whole day off from school. To cheer us both up, we stopped by a thrift store on the way to her appointment—an antique-y place in our town that we'd never been to, but we had admired for years. The thought hung in the air between us; *bone cancer was terminal*, and we might never get another chance to go.

The creaky store smelled of stale cigar smoke, with a twinge of alcohol. My mother and I wandered around the packed aisles together, looking at bashful Kewpie dolls, Patsy Cline record albums and hand-sewn leather wallets, while the owner invited us to donate towards his electric bill. He was a large, Grizzly Adams-type, with an open bottle of booze, so I wasn't going to give him any money. I spotted a basket of old-fashioned children's books—the small size that cost 29 cents in the '60s.

I dug around in the basket.

"I never did find that old mouse book..."

My mother laughed.

"Look in your hand."

I'd grabbed a perfect copy of *Timmy Mouse*, his cherub face still familiar to me after 30 years.

My skin tingled. It was a sign. I felt it as sure as the book in my hand. And I knew. At that very moment, I knew in my soul that my mother would live, that *I* would too.

I wish I could say that the book had my name in it, from all those years before, but it didn't. I'd grown up in a city a couple hours away, and that would have been very unlikely. Even so, finding the book and the happy ending in the story was a blessing, and I could feel it blanket me in a soft protection.

I clutched the book and went to Grizzly Adams to pay for it. The original price was still there, but this was an antique store. It would probably be expensive.

"How much is this little book?"

"How much ya got?" Grizzly asked.

I frowned. People were only allowed to say that in the movies. I waited.

"It's twelve bucks. You got twelve bucks?"

"I do." I handed him the cash.

"How about the electric bill? You got some for that?"

"I don't."

I rushed my mom to the car and I shoved *Timmy Mouse* into her hands.

"Read it! Read it to me."

"What? *You're* the teacher," she said. "*You* read it."

She clearly didn't take this moment to heart as much as I did.

"No, I want to hear it in your *mommy* voice, like when I was little. Do it now, before I get in your lap. And say all the good parts the way as you *used* to."

Amazing how all the best lines came right back to me. I made her read it twice through, and I would have asked for a third, but we were running late.

I drove us to her oncology appointment, with the little book in my lap. I needed to get some on me, some of its blessed happy ending.

When we arrived, the doctor opened my mother's file.

"Oh, yes! Mmmm. You're the one. You don't have cancer. Not bone cancer. Not any cancer. Go on now. Get out of my office. I've got sick people to see."

He was a funny oncologist.

A mistake in diagnosis, maybe? A miracle? A stay of execution? Since she was my mother, I received it as a miracle. That's what I would tell her later when she asked for my thoughts on what had happened to her.

I looked the doctor in the eye. He had soft, brown eyes. He nodded and smiled with a deep understanding of the loss that passed over me. I threw my arms around him in a silent thank you.

"You're welcome," he said. "You have lots of years together. Take care of your mom."

And I did. I took her to my house. She was warm, blue-eyed, and *alive*! We sat on the couch, my mom on one side of me, my boy on the other, and I read *Timmy Mouse* to our three generations. A celebration, although by then, my boy was much too cool for the story. Not having a sibling, a broken family, or a newly living mother, he didn't identify with the mice like I had.

But many of my students would. On the last day of school, sore throat flaring, I read that book. For nearly a year, these kids had been mine. I'd tried to give them the security that was so crucial to me, back when the most important thing was just coming home to "mouse house."

During the last minutes with my students, I stopped being tired of their behavior and their parents, stopped wishing the year away, and savored the story that I loved so much.

"Mrs. M., it's good those mice found their family and went home together."

"You're sort of like our family, Mrs. M."

Some of us cried.

My students agreed to live happily ever after, and they left my classroom for the last time.

Reading that story was my gift to them, a blessing over them, as it had been for me. Some of them were a gift for me.

"How much ya got?" the thrift store Grizzly Adams had asked.

I took a quick inventory. My mother wasn't sick anymore. Teaching wasn't using up my emotional and mental cushioning. I had skin left, and guts. I had patience, creativity, determination—and now another year of experience.

I could teach a third year.

16
A Temporary Life

On the first day of summer, I woke up at the same time as a school day, but without the blaring alarm. I lay wiggling my toes in the soft sheets and mentally making sure I had the day off. Yes, yesterday had been the last day of school.

Today, it was summer, and none of those kids were mine anymore. Thankfully, that year's Humper was someone else's problem now. Poor Bella and her lost cat; I'd never know what happened to it. I'd forgotten to write a note home about Avery's ear ache. Too late! The sudden change must be like death. I gave death a lot of thought after my mother was spared.

I fluffed my pillow and imagined the end of my own life. There would be a mandatory awards assembly in heaven's auditorium. Mrs. Hill, who'd fired me from student teaching, would play the part of God—she'd like that. She'd stand at the podium and call me to the stage, where I'd receive loud applause for my participation in the Human Experience.

Mrs. Hill would present me with ribbons for my accomplishments: the Good Girl Ribbon; a Writer's Ribbon, and the You Got Fired Ribbon. She'd smirk at the word "fired." And then, grudgingly, she'd hand me my Teacher's Ribbon. Yes, she would hand it over. To me. I'd be gracious though, and not jerk it out of her hand or call her something vile. I'd be *thinking* it, though.

I got up and washed my face, but I stayed in my jammies, happy to be home. My very being was molded to the whirlwind shape of school, kids, plastic scissors, a dwindling supply of construction paper, a militant daily schedule, and aching feet. All of it consumed my thoughts. Then, in one moment, it was over. For a few days, I was lost without the classroom.

I couldn't write my husband's name on our kitchen message board as a punishment—or maybe I could. I'd try it.

My own child was eager to eat mom-made macaroni and cheese and to leave his dish for me to pick up. My dog, Chester, needed to be petted and told how handsome he was. I had to build a different life now, for the summer. A temporary life.

Because the days of school would indeed return; I'd signed a contract. It was a contract on my own life, or ten months of it, and I played in its shadow all summer.

The structure of a summer day, though, was comfortably loose: I slept until my body wanted to wake up, had complete thoughts all my own, and time. That raw sore throat quickly disappeared, with no lingering symptoms. I retrained myself to use the bathroom instead of waiting until lunchtime. I read for pleasure, and my feet and back stopped hurting within days.

I spent plenty of guilt-free time with my mom, newly given back to me. The cancer cloud was gone from over our heads. I wasn't obligated to be anywhere.

Some teachers chose to work the summer school program or find a short term nanny job for cash, but I melted into the social break. I needed it.

Students were out for eight weeks. Teachers were out for six—we boxed up the classrooms and took an inventory at the end of the school year, and then we'd set everything back up in the fall. Forty-two days of home, soft T-shirts and cotton shorts, few appointments, and a life without that sea of eyes!

One summer day, starving and looking unprofessional in flip flops, I dashed into the grocery store for chips and salsa. A growling father walked up to me, entered my large bubble of personal space and folded his arms across his chest.

"Mrs. M., I see you're using my tax dollars for doing nothing all summer. That doesn't seem fair."

I stood mute, trying to find the articulate, appropriate version of my brain. I felt like I'd been caught cheating on a test.

"We don't get paid for the summer."

I was unsure if I even owed him an explanation.

"Owen Charter withholds paychecks and puts them aside."

And I never forgot that privilege.

Before I ever taught at Owen Charter, and years before I'd taught preschool, I worked at a daycare for six dollars an hour, 11 hours a day. I filled in the money gaps by babysitting overnight or on weekends.

The other daycare workers and I ate perfectly good food that the kids threw away—nothing gross, just a clean whole apple or a sealed box of animal cookies. A perfect pack of gummy bears was hard to leave in the trash. Kids threw away a lot of food, and not every parent wanted it back.

To be a teacher now, with money earned and time leftover, I was a princess in a castle.

"But you leave school at three o'clock, every day. You *owe* me those hours."

I couldn't *believe* some kid's father was confronting me! Teachers couldn't leave at three o'clock. Most of the kids weren't even picked up until four-thirty. He had no idea what the job was like, what my life was like.

I waved and walked on, later wishing I had told him about all the teaching requirements I had to fulfill each summer, all the classes I took towards renewing my certificate.

Owen Charter required a huge merit project, comparing standardized test scores to improve my success. I read more books on new teaching methods and discipline strategies.

I imagined that mean dad confronting Mrs. Hill, and fighting it out. She would have put him right down to the ground in a choke hold of words and left him doubting the existence of his own testicles! I smiled. Maybe Mrs. Hill was good for something, after all.

I wondered what she would think if she could see me at Owen Charter, with the "trash teachers" as she'd called them. I doubted she had the skills to work with the impoverished parents and aggressive students at Owen Charter, and do it all while she thought her mother was dying of cancer.

I was sure Mrs. Hill lacked the creativity to teach with few supplies, limited books, and still turn out kids who loved to read. Mrs. Hill might have strong opinions, but she wasn't willing to try hard. She certainly hadn't tried very hard to mentor me.

It was time I got over her, to quit letting her occupy my thoughts. She had been my workplace bully and nothing more. I decided to stop eating hate-flavored candy, with its creamy grudge filling.

I tried instead to think of Mrs. Hill clearly. Even though my experience with her had been negative, there were students who responded well to her style. And if it weren't for her firing me, I might never have known Mrs. Gardener.

By telling me I might never be a teacher, Mrs. Hill forced me to prove her wrong. And I did. Struggling until success came—that was my area of expertise.

I drove home, scarfed some chips and salsa and put away the groceries. There was laundry to throw in the washer and an online class to study for. I breathed in the scent of home: linen-scented carpet powder, maple syrup and pancakes dishes from breakfast, the ink smell of a book in my hands.

This was the life!

The Third Year

17
How to Use a Pencil

When I was a child, I wanted my own pencil with a sharp point, and I didn't share or borrow. Other kids couldn't be trusted with my pencil; their touch left an invisible mark that felt intrusive. I insisted that my mother peel a small rectangle of paint from a new pencil and write my name on it in ink.

As a teacher, I hadn't anticipated what a problem pencils could be in a classroom of small children. Pencils were grimy things that had to be disinfected, sharpened, distributed, collected and re-sharpened, many times a day.

The kids could not use the pencil sharpener by themselves, or the goal in class became breaking and sharpening down to nubs rather than learning. They would have happily drowned out my attempts at instruction with the loud grinding noise.

Owen Charter had a school policy: Teachers were to sharpen enough pencils to fill a large coffee can—a morning's supply. The can was kept in the back of the room and sharpened again at lunch.

During my third year teaching, a young mother volunteered in my classroom. Mrs. Ellis had come from Mexico and spoke the English language perfectly, without slang. It was pleasant to hear her at a time when Owen Charter parents were toddlerizing the language.

"My son jump-ted off his bunk bed" or "Me and him went to the store."

In Arizona, close to the Mexico border, we often had immigrant students and their Spanish speaking parents. I'd been required to take two English Immersion classes for my teacher's certification. Because Mrs. Ellis spoke both languages so beautifully, I invited her to give a social studies talk.

She'd grown up in a remote village and married a missionary. Her given name, Tavi, meant "pretty flower" in her native dialect. She described eating corn mush three times a day as a child. Her morning bath was a bucket of river water over her head, and she knew eleven different games to play, using only a handful of smooth stones.

I would have had a problem with the corn mush and river water plumbing, but in some ways, I envied that peaceful and self-contained life. In another culture, I might have had fewer anxiety triggers.

"School for me was a small hut, with a dirt floor," she told us. "Each child received, from the teacher, one pencil to last all of our school days. *One* pencil!"

"One pencil each year?" I asked.

I wanted my first graders to understand the privilege they had as Americans.

"No, Mrs. M.," she smiled, embarrassed at correcting a teacher. "One pencil for our *entire* education."

"Boys and girls," I said, "We can't make a pencil last the morning, and Mrs. Ellis made hers last for years!"

"What if you broke it?" asked one of the girls.

"I would not break my pencil. It was a prize to me, and there would never be another one."

Mrs. Ellis changed the way I thought about pencils. They were tools of education and, without them, written communication would be difficult. I felt guilty for throwing away our destroyed ones and opening a new box every couple days.

Even more timid than I was, Mrs. Ellis was a safe person, and kindred to me. I refused to miss out on her experiences, due to our mutual quietness, so I begged for more stories.

Her village sounded like a paradise, with quiet time, sweet friendships and children who took such good care of their belongings that they lasted a lifetime. It became my mental happy place.

"It is hard for me to speak with you, Mrs. M."

The class was at recess.

"Your eye contact lasts too long for me."

I was shocked. It was stressful for me to make eye contact when my social anxiety was flaring. I had trained myself to do it because it is expected in American culture. After that, Mrs. Ellis and I did our chatting while cutting paper for art projects.

I convinced her to set up a pen-pal correspondence with her village school. Hopefully, the project would last all year, and I could continue to enjoy her company. My class drew pictures of people smiling, and we copied a sentence in her language from the board. We sent a package of new pencils, and we never heard back.

"My village spurns Western culture. I'm afraid they were offended by your letters and your pencils," she said.

I could relate to that; I was offended by our pencils, too.

"But you are a fine teacher, Mrs. M.," she assured me.

I appreciated her for admiring my skill; I'd worked hard for it. In her honor, I tried to teach my students respect for our valuable pencils, to use them with care, or at least not to destroy them deliberately.

Rather than cherishing their abundance, many of my students seemed to take a sinister joy in ruining what they had. It seemed Owen Charter kids didn't understand the concept of "one and no more."

By my third year in the classroom, I was becoming territorial. The *room* was mine! The *stuff in it* was mine. I wanted to write "Mrs. M." on all the pencils and clutch the coffee can to my chest.

Instead, I wrote a poem. I never read it to the students or posted it in the classroom, but I was tempted. I called it *How to Use A Pencil*, by Mrs. M.:

Tell your teacher you need a pencil.

Break off the eraser.
Crimp the metal end with your teeth.
Chew and swallow the metal end.
Tell your teacher what you've done.

Scrape the paint off your pencil with your scissors.
Bite all the way around it to create lumps.
You might be in trouble for that.
Hide your pencil.

Tell your teacher you need a pencil.

Poke a kid sitting close to you with it.
Be prepared to deny it.
Break off the pencil lead and write with that.
Smash the wooden end flat. Say it was an accident.

Grind a hole into your desktop.
Gather a lot of pencils to make a good hole.
Hoard pencils in the back of your desk.

You have a lot of them. Break one in half.

Never have a pencil when you're asked to write.
Borrow another child's pencil and don't give it back.
Tell your teacher that kid stole yours.
Don't let her see inside your desk.

Tell your teacher you need a pencil.

If you're a little girl, put a nice long pencil up your nose.
Freud would love that.
If you're a boy, use a pencil to scratch your butt.
Then smell it.

Ask your mom to buy a certain brand of pencil.
Have her put your name on it with red glitter ink.
Better still, bring a sparkly pencil from home and taunt others with it.
Cry when it gets stolen.

Refuse any pencil except one that is pristinely new.
You have your standards.
Sharpen your brand new pencil all the way down to the tiniest nub.
Call it adorable.

Shove a pencil into the skin between your fingers.
Let the pencil hang there.
Scrape a hole in your skin with a freshly sharpened pencil.
Ask to see the nurse.

Fold your eyelid around your pencil.

Try to write that way.
Poke a pencil into the corner of your eye.
Say you just wanted to see what would happen.

Weave the pencil through your fingers.
Then spin it on your pointer finger.
Use your large pink eraser to catapult your pencil across the room.
This works best during a test.

Tell your teacher you need a pencil.

****

Documenting my struggles made me stronger, and I stopped gritting my teeth at the snap of every writing tool.

One day, my student, Katelyn, stayed in for recess to correct a math test.

"Oh, I get it now!" she said, and erased gently so the paper didn't tear.

"See my pencil? I keep it nice for my assignments like you said, Mrs. M."

I thought of Mrs. Ellis's village, where I should have been born, where life was pure and pencils were holy. Katelyn was one of us.

"Then let me write your name on that pencil," I said, "so it can be your own."

Mrs. Ellis would be proud of us.

18
A Day in the Classroom

During my third year of teaching, I noticed the crackling nerves were growing quieter, softer. I'd never fainted at Owen Charter—hadn't since student teaching—and I no longer looked at teaching with dreamy or even scared eyes. I was able to see with clarity how immense the job was.

I arrived at Owen Charter at seven-thirty each morning to set up for the first activity and meet with any parents who needed to talk. Sometimes a parent dropped off a homework folder and said something cheery like, "I wish I was a teacher. This would be a fun, easy job."

One morning, the conversation was more ominous.

"Mrs. M., I'm sorry to bother you, but my husband left me last night for another woman. Kenzie was in the room, listening to the whole thing, so she might need a little extra attention today."

"Oh, I'm so sorry."

I hugged this mother. I spent my days with her child and felt her shock like it was my own. I spoke to Kenzie.

"You picked a good day to come to school early, because I need some help in here."

"I'm wearing dirty pants," mumbled Kenzie, "and my daddy left."

"Your pants look fine for a school day. Can you take all the chairs off the desks?"

I let the mother talk a while longer, but at eight-thirty, the class came in and instruction had to begin, no matter what.

Anytime I met with parents or had a phone call, I documented the date and the conversation in a file. I made sure that every report card and progress note was signed. I'd learned the hard way that some parents will agree, even in writing, to retain their struggling child in first grade for another year, and later claim that they thought he or she was an A student.

By the time I corralled 30 kids to hang up backpacks, set out homework, say the pledge and sit for attendance, the morning was well under way. I announced the first assignment.

"Boys and girls, it is time for our spelling test."

We reviewed the words and studied the tricky spellings, pretending to draw the letters on the movie screens behind our eyes. I moved desks and distributed privacy screens to prevent copying. First graders were expert cheaters.

"Write your name on your paper. Keep your eyes on your own work and use your neatest handwriting. Your paper should be neat, sweet and complete."

"And don't wipe snot on them," some child always called out, "because you have to grade these on your kitchen table tonight, right Mrs. M.?"

I'd said that once in frustration, and they never let me forget it. I began the test.

"Number one: Mouse. Mouse. Jaden has a pet mouse with a gray tail. Mouse. Word number one is mouse." I walked around and praised students for correct letter formation and spelling. I warned some to think again, to look at the alphabet on the wall and make sure their letter "S" faced the S direction.

I replaced broken pencils, handed out several tissues and wrote kids' names on the board for talking, and then I went on to word number two. The test took about 45 minutes; we had 30 words a week in first grade. I enjoyed giving a test and seeing real progress. I could watch the evidence of their learning appear on the papers.

Sometimes, the mornings included an "observer." The nervous feelings reappeared like an overdue bill. Sweat dotted my upper lip and I talked too fast and too squeaky. Principal Owen, parents, student teachers, someone from the Department of Education, or total strangers could observe a classroom for an hour or even the rest of the day, unscheduled if they wanted to— people with no expertise or experience with children were free to evaluate any teacher's performance.

Despite the unwelcome nerves, I knew how to make myself *look* like an effective and competent teacher, a professional. I slowed myself down. I was careful to have children in their seats, a calm voice, a hands-on activity ready, instead of a worksheet.

I called on children in the back row frequently. Being watched for improvement made me feel ashamed, like a puppy having her nose rubbed into the pee-soaked carpet. But observations went with the job and happened to all teachers.

It was kind of funny, really, what people tried to change. Our kindergarten teacher had an observer complain that she dressed too *nicely* to work with children. Another mother pulled her daughter out of Owen Charter, because she felt that too many of the teachers "had gotten fat." I myself had once been described as "irresponsible-looking." I guess I wasn't wearing enough lipstick that day.

One morning, Mrs. Edwards, who was the wife of a prominent citizen in town, popped in unannounced, to see if she wanted to enroll their little girl, Camden, at the school. My class happened to be baking sugar cookies from scratch as a lesson in reading recipes. I loved a crazy distraction, and I was proud to show off my creativity and organizational skills. This was above and beyond required curriculum.

I'd pre-enlisted three trustworthy parent volunteers, who were not germophobes or gossips, to lead a group of seven or eight students, while following my directions. I'd made four stations out of sanitized desks that were each fully equipped with a bowl, measuring spoons and all ingredients.

Sometimes, parents would donate ingredients and sometimes I bought them with my own money. I rewrote recipes to make a "small-batch" and practiced them at home first. That way each group made just enough.

I always kept the recipe on my station and called out directions to the parents who were leading groups. It never worked to give parents a copy of the recipe, because one of them would be done in three minutes with bored kids, one would be overwhelmed with kids and not cooking at all, and the third would mess up the recipe so that it had to be done over again. I made sure to have extra ingredients in case of disasters.

The student groups were important for the success of the recipe. An out-of-control group would ruin it for everyone. On paper, I'd divided the class into four groups, based upon separating personality conflicts, having a very shy student in each group, and some who followed directions well.

Some students needed to be watched closely for things such as stealing ingredients, sneezing or coughing, and nose picking; I put one of those in each group.

I'd met with the parent helpers prior to the project and discussed the process with them. The parents were to measure the ingredients, one at a time, as I announced them, and then let the students take turns pouring it in the bowl.

Each student would get a turn to pour and a turn to stir. Turns could be revoked due to any reason, from attitude to sneezing in the bowl. The question of germs always came up, and I reminded parents cheerfully that the cookies would be baked at a high temperature.

Soon, the room smelled sweet and each station had a bowl of finished cookie dough. I was sure my observing mom was impressed. The children had been well-behaved and were now studiously spooning two balls of gritty white dough onto tin foil squares.

On each square, I had pre-written a child's name in Sharpie ink, which survives baking. I'd brought extra cookie sheets from home, because the ones in the school kitchen were always lost on the day of the cooking project.

When baked and cool, the cookies were either eaten by students just prior to dismissal or taken home in a pre-labeled zippy bag; most girls wanted to give their cookies to their moms. Principal Owen often followed the smell of baking cookies, so I made her a pretty one and let the class present it to her. She'd bravely eat the whole cookie, make "yum" sounds, quiz a child on the ingredients and leave us to finish our activity.

Little Camden and Mrs. Edwards had observed our entire cooking process, so I gave them some cookies to eat and invited them to pull up a chair and visit with us.

Later, Mrs. Edwards left a message on the school answering machine for anyone to overhear.

"Mrs. M. could have done a better job with that cookie activity. I guess the old saying is true: Those who can't *do*—teach."

An ugly word came into my mind.

I wanted to see this accuser make sugar cookies from scratch with 30 kids, three parent helpers, and an observer. I had a tougher skin by then, but Mrs. Edwards' comment punctured.

I didn't know of any other job where people outside the profession could follow employees around and say they were doing it wrong. After a few of these observers, I stopped trying so hard to impress them. I reasoned that I already had 30 kids. Did I really want another?

Usually, a morning was spent in less flamboyant reading activities, such as the phonemic drills of pairing letters with sounds. Reading groups were always a favorite of mine.

Most days, I had a 40-minute lunch break to sit with Mrs. Gardener and cackle over the crazy morning, discussing what worked and didn't work with certain students. Sometimes I was called to talk to a parent or Principal Owen.

The kids went to recess, but if there was rain, snow, or temperatures below 40 degrees, they had to stay in the classroom with me. My feet and back ached, but I was up for the challenge. Often, instead of lunch, I'd drink some cold water, shove a cheese stick in my mouth, and keep going.

After lunch, I settled the kids in with a story; I preferred a good fairy tale. I could read *The Three Bears* every day for the rest of my life and feel a deep sense of belonging. The cozy house, the warm oatmeal, and the "just-rightness" of a midafternoon nap pulled me into their pages.

A lively session of behavior training fit well in the afternoons. Many kids at Owen Charter spent their entire days with a long succession of adults, who were not parents. It was the teacher during the day, and then after-school staff until a babysitter picked them up, and then they spent the night at dad's girlfriend's apartment.

Lots of schools featured character development in order to teach values that students didn't get at home. It went deeper than manners, which we taught continually anyway. Behavior training was my contribution, and it helped kids to take a look at their own choices. I started by telling them we were going to do some *thinking*.

I hated having to call everything a "game." Would they also play a "driving game" when they turned 16 and wanted a license? Not everything in life was a game, and neither was this. It was using a moral compass, but I'd be in trouble for going too far with that.

On the board, I wrote two activities the kids knew well: class and recess. Then I asked for suggestions on ways we should behave at recess. We made a list: run, scream, play and slide. Then we made another list for behaviors that were okay during class: read, raise our hands, work quietly and listen.

I asked them what was different about the two. Was it okay to scream in the classroom? Did we need to raise our hands on the playground? Of course not! These places were different and the expected behavior was different.

We went on to compare other activities: church and a football game, a friend's house and the lunchroom.

"Now is the time to change your behavior, *before* you have consequences."

I told them to think about expectations in other places too.

"Do you *want* to get in trouble at the grocery store? Then how do you act there?"

I found that the behavior in my classes improved with this training. Sometimes, we had refresher trainings and reminders. All I had to say was: "Where are you right now?" It helped some kids to think ahead, prevent problems and display some social grace.

Math also came in the early afternoon, and first graders were tired by that time, inattentive, and full of the sugary crap from their lunchboxes.

"Flynn, this is math time. Where *are* you right now? Learning in school. Let's not play with things in our desks. Class, use the connecting blocks I gave you to make a tower of six blocks. Six. I said six. Now add two more. How many blocks do we have now? Stella, those aren't yours. Give them back. That's right, we have eight blocks. Class, take away four blocks from your tower. Back in your seat, Flynn! And how many blocks do we have now? Jamie, put your shoes on. Yes, we have four left. Let's use our blocks to help us add and subtract on our worksheet."

Afternoons felt like training squirrels, and I wondered how much math they were learning.

We played a lot of bingo in first grade—gambling adapted to academic subjects. It was a fun way to sneak in some review of any subject, from reading to spelling to math. The bingo game pieces were red cardboard circles, and the kids immediately ate, ripped, rolled, or stole the ones that came with the box, ruining yet another teaching tool I'd purchased with my own money.

I considered buying plastic bingo chips, but they were expensive. Plus, anything shiny or pink was sure to be stolen. Ink stampers would render the games useless for another day. I thought about small pebbles, but the school had a zero tolerance policy on rocks and related items. The Dollar Store sold bags of little shells and glass discs, all swallowing hazards.

Then I had a moment of genius: tiny puzzle pieces—the kind that came in those thousand-piece puzzles. They were the perfect size to mark a bingo square, and I could get puzzles labeled "missing pieces" free from the thrift store. When the kids ruined or stole them, I didn't have to feel the loss from my own pocket.

My own careless attitude about the puzzle pieces translated to the children taking on the responsibility. They were protective of those mismatched puzzle pieces.

"Teacher," they'd say solemnly, holding out a crumpled wad of cardboard. "We found this on the floor." As if the puzzle pieces were ever worth more than the trash.

Aside from the bingo, all this teaching produced daily stacks of assignments that required cheery stickers and smiley ink stamps. From spelling tests to math homework, everything needed some kind of mark, even if it came from a bright ink pen.

Mostly, I was enthusiastic about buying cute incentives for the class. I'd picture the students, their brows furrowed over a test. Other times, there were bills at home that needed paying, and I thought twice about expenses of the job.

Parents contributed basics to the classroom, such as Kleenex and crayons, but the class library belonged to me. We teachers were responsible for buying the posters, the alphabet, rainy day games and gift supplies so the kids could make mom and dad something for Christmas.

We paid for the name tags on the desks, notebooks and folders and more, when those wore out. We filled the prize box with cute pencils and plastic rings. Many Owen Charter families couldn't afford to buy what the kids needed for school—so *we* did. It cost a lot to be a teacher, and not much was tax deductible.

The teacher's day was not the short, six hours of fun that I remembered so fondly from my own childhood. Teachers had never been allowed to leave at three o'clock. But when the economy worsened, Owen Charter salaries were lowered and the day was lengthened. I was disappointed and tired, but there was nothing I could do about it.

Instead of preparing projects and supplies for the next day, we were required to earn back our money by leading afterschool activities. It was hard to adjust to giving up my prep time. That had been soothing time alone, or in camaraderie with my teaching buddy, Mrs. Gardener.

Now, I tutored struggling readers while she counseled troubled kids. Other teachers coached volleyball or loaded a couple hundred kids into an endless line of cars.

At about four o'clock, I was finally free to breathe. This became my time to ready the room, grade papers and return phone calls to parents. Occasionally, there was a meeting—school-wide or grade-level, IEPs for struggling or disabled students, parent-conferences or a workshop. Teachers were known to complain, but I secretly enjoyed the adult contact and the little vacation for my feet.

At one of these meetings, Principal Owen made an announcement.

"Due to expenses and the poor economy, we've laid off our janitorial service."

I didn't like the direction this was going.

"Enlist some *parent* volunteers!" Mrs. Gardener called out.

"Do not—*do not* request parent volunteers for cleaning duty," warned Principal Owen. "We don't want them pulling kids out because they think we're financially unstable... or lazy."

"Student helpers?" I called out. It was a fair suggestion, and I was not ashamed of it.

"Cleaning substances are toxic," said Principal Owen. "I have purchased supplies for teachers only. Please plan time at the end of each day to sweep up the piles of grit in your rooms, mop your floors and empty the trashcans. You can take turns sanitizing the student bathrooms. Sorry about all the pee on the walls."

"This is *crazy!*" we mouthed to each other.

I imagined the open juice boxes and containers of milk that had leaked into a sticky puddle over my floor that day. Mopping it myself, I gained a new respect for the people in our former janitorial service.

I figured I'd had it pretty easy until then: I had a nice routine, and first grade was running smoothly for me. Until then, I'd been leaving around five-thirty, tired but satisfied with the ten-hour day.

There were also weekly lesson plans, a parent newsletter to write and a class statistics book to keep, so two or three nights a week, I took work home. Once a month, progress reports or report cards took a weekend.

It was exhausting, but I'd earned the right with my own sweat and nerves. I'd earned the right to do so many different tasks with confidence. I was proud of the exhaustion. It marked me as a good teacher.

What I used to fear, I did now with strength—not all the time, but I felt capable. The old, "scared me" was not a shed skin, useless and left behind. She was tucked away inside, shielded from harm. I had joined the club of established teachers, and so I pitched in to clean the rooms of the overwhelmed new teachers—big sister style.

Mrs. Gardener liked to say, "We might have enough time to get the job done, if we didn't have to teach children."

She could teach any child with nothing but a little time. I wanted to be like Mrs. Gardener. I wanted to make teaching look like a fun, easy job.

19
Sneaker and Three

Names were a hobby of mine, and the classroom provided me with a year's worth at a time. After teaching preschool, and being in my third year at Owen Charter, I'd seen plenty of names. I could sit back and enjoy this part of the job.

For kids, names were a source of embarrassment or the envy of others. The girls I knew growing up had names like Debbie, Shelly, Heidi and Mandy. The "ee" sound at the end was considered cute and feminine in '70s American culture. These were recognizable *human* names.

Just about the only weird thing that happened back then was when parents decided to combine mom's name with dad's to create a new one for the child. Tim and Marie became Timarie. Rodney and Jane was Rodja. June and Lanny: Julani. Or if the parents were hippies, they named a girl after a beautiful flower, like Hyacinth.

"Why did you name me Carrie?" I'd often asked my mother.

I didn't like my name. Carrie rhymed with fairy, which was not a compliment. More importantly, it was not popular, so I couldn't get fun stuff with my name on it, like a license plate for my bike or a rainbow sign for my bedroom door.

"I named you after a friend of mine," she said, as if that might change my mind.

"Who?" I asked, unable to picture this family friend.

"Oh, her name was Carol or something like that. I don't really remember."

It didn't help to be named after someone who wasn't important enough to stay in touch with. I discovered that my name was in the top 25 in the late 1800s, but so were Fannie and Myrtle.

An eccentric old lady at church was named Carrie. My mom and I used to visit her, because it was Christian to visit old ladies from church. Old lady Carrie lived in a silver trailer that was dark inside and smelled of moth balls.

She told me I could watch her television. It was a tiny black-and-white set that got one channel. The *Munsters* was the only thing on, and that show was scary—which also rhymed with Carrie. Each time we visited, she let me take one penny from her penny jar as a special treat. Even as a child, that didn't impress me.

Then came Stephen King's movie, *Carrie.* I'd watched the movie trailers on TV—the blood and the screaming. None of the kids at school had actually seen the movie, which was rated R in the '70s, but I hated the comments.

"You look just like her!"

"Can we have your autograph?"

As an adult, I finally worked up the nerve to read the book. I should have read it before becoming a teacher. I think I'd have avoided schools all together and saved myself a lot of trouble.

In junior high, a boy named Anthony Berry liked me. I didn't know him well, but I heard rumors that he wanted to "go" with me. We could hold hands and pass notes, things like that.

Just to be on the safe side, pre-"going" status, I tried my name with his: Carrie Berry. I decided he needn't approach me. Unfortunately, I wasn't the only one who put names together, and there was no end to the rhymes after that. Hairy Carrie, Carrie's cherry and Carrie from the Dairy.

After the kind of treachery I'd had with my own name, I felt sorry for the students at Owen Charter, whose parents seemed to name them so haphazardly. I expected modern parents to be a little more aware of the potential for teasing, having lived through it themselves. But we teachers did have the advantage of seeing name trends and trying them out for a year.

The name "Caden" was popular at our school since I'd started working there. Teachers had three or four Cadens in every class.

Parents seemed to object to having too many children with *their* child's name, as if his individuality were being stolen. This started the name rhyming, which was already a peeve of mine. Caden became Jaden, Brayden and Hayden.

Suddenly, any human name had a string of rhymes. Maia, Kaia, Shya—Carlie, Harleigh and Charlee. Gnarly would have been cute.

Kylie turned into Rylie, Mylie and Brylie. Haley became Bailee, Zailey and Jailie. I pictured the limited career options for an adult with that name. No one would hire a defense attorney named Jailie. The attempts at uniqueness were endless, and spellings became tricky. I kept my class lists handy when writing desk tags or completing paperwork at the beginning of the year.

A different trend began as Michaela, and quickly mutated into the McName: McKayla, McKyla, McKenna and McCreigh. I could only imagine the McDonald's menu of teasing I would have had to tolerate if that had been my name.

An action-figure series of names brought us boys called Race, Scout, Duke and Ridge. Then came the nature names: Winter, Briar, Meadow and Koala. I expected some weird spelling with Koala—K-a-W-a-l-l-a or some such. But no, the child I knew was just regular Koala.

President names were popular for a while: Reagan, Carter, Kennedy, Madison and Grover. *Grover*. Although I never heard anyone tease that child about the Sesame Street character, I was tempted to myself from time to time.

Some parents gave a boy the mother's maiden name: Cooper, Walker or McIntyre. Brady was cute on the right kid. I knew a child with a hyphenated set of names to honor both families. His first name was Evans-Wilson.

Foreign names were tricky. A lovely Swedish mother named her boy Gunner. The problem was she wanted us to pronounce it in her native dialect, "Gooner." This caused widespread teasing.

Principal Owen had a discreet talk with the mother and explained that the word "goon" had unpleasant connotations in American slang. The mother compromised by having us call the child by his middle name, Lane.

Sometimes, kids' names reflected parents' jobs or hobbies. A pair of brothers in my class were Micah and Cole, but spelled M-i-c-a and C-o-a-l. Their dad was a geologist. A firefighter mom named her kids Ash, Ember and Blaze. A book-lover named her girls Paige and Reed. A drummer's boy was Cadence. I heard of a rodeo fan, who named his boys Rider and Roper, except Rider liked to rope and Roper liked to ride.

I wondered at this trend in names. While Americans named a cute little baby something precious, some parents seemed unaware that their child would one day become an adult. For me, social interactions were difficult enough without have to distinguish regular words from names. I found myself relishing the plain human names on my roster: Gracie, Lydia, Cyrus and Hiram.

I found it intriguing when a set of parents would name their first child something wildly creative, like Cassiopeia Star, and name their second child simply, Ann. Did the family's preferences change that much in the two or three years between children, or did they tire of yelling all those syllables across the backyard?

We had a lot of romantic names at Owen Charter: Story, Ever, Memory, Journey, Promise, Serenity— Serendipity, as her adult half-sister called her.

Map names became a trend: Montana, Cheyenne, Berlin, Topanga, and even North and West. Teenage mothers seemed to pick Disney names for their babies, like Bella, Ariel and Jasmine. Occasionally, we had virtuous names like Patience, Purity and Trinity, but they seemed out of place at a rather behavioral school like Owen Charter.

Some parents chose a portion of the alphabet and named their children consecutively: Avery, Blake and Claire. Then, if a name they preferred didn't fit, they forced it in. D'Laura was the next child. A teacher friend told me about a family she knew who skipped the creative process altogether and named their child ABCD, pronounced *Absidy*.

There was a brief attempt at lovely words, spelled backwards. "Heaven" was reversed to Nevaeh. I had a coworker who planned to name her baby Evol, or love spelled backwards.

She changed her mind, however, when she saw her beautiful child for the first time and didn't want the pronunciation mistaken for Evil. I was relieved this trend didn't catch on. Most pretty words were too hard to pronounce backwards.

Affluent mothers seemed to give their children long, tedious names. Twins, Gabriella and Priscilla, belonged to a prominent doctor in town. It took seven syllables to get their attention, and the mother cautioned us teachers not to use "diminutives" when referring to her daughters. It seemed to be her way of infringing upon my time as a reminder of their superior worth.

In the believe-it-or-not category, I had a child in class whose baby brother was legally named "Damn." His father's name was Damien, and they shortened it by removing a couple of vowels. Everyone was duly horrified, which was the exact response the parents were hoping for. I imagined the child with his mother in the grocery line.

"Damn, put that candy back. We're not buying it. Damn!"

Teachers had an informal meeting to discuss the problem. We could not use the name Damn in the classroom. Other children, those taught not to swear, would be offended and report misunderstandings at home.

"Mommy, Mrs. M. keeps telling Damn to turn in his homework. Is she cussing?"

We decided, if any of us were still working at Owen Charter by the time the child reached our grades, that we would call him by his initials, D. S. The Damn child seemed sickly too, as if cursed.

When I worked in preschool, I noticed the kids had a hard time with names. Three-year-olds were still trying to make sense of the world, and they applied meaning where there was none. The kids called Olivia "I love ya." Mackenzie's friends called her "I can't see." A boy named Pearson was enrolled, and the kids tattled on "Person."

I liked that idea, just labeling people something that fit. It seemed organized and rather soothing. I wished for a class full of kids named Helper, with the occasional Brat thrown in for flavor, and I would be Mrs. Nice. Names could be prophetic, though, and we had a preschooler named Rowdy. He liked to climb the structures on the playground and pee on the kids below.

Another girl in my class came from a family of all females. Her mother, a teenage sister, and the child were all named Ella-Marie. I wondered if the mother ever got confused and about how they managed their phone calls. Was their cat a girl, and if so, was she also named Ella-Marie?

In the first grade, names were especially important because I required them to be written on every single paper. Then the kids wrote them on desks, arms and shoes, which was punishable by cleaning them off.

First graders sometimes came across a name in one of the older textbooks used at Owen Charter. Most of the books we had were purchased in the '80s, and they were generations older than the kids using them.

"What does Sharon mean?" a child would ask.

I started explaining to them ahead of time that Sharon was a girl's name, or Chuck was a boy's name.

Just for fun, I took an informal poll of teachers and asked for the weirdest names they'd ever had in class. The girls' list included Butterfly, Silky, Jello and Midgett. The boys were Rampage, Rocket and a set of twins, named Sneaker and Three.

Judging by these names, children and pets have switched places in the family. Dogs and cats used to answer to Fluffy and Spot, but now they receive older human names, like Max and Molly. I named my dog after our great grandpa, Chester—a name no longer suitable for children because it rhymes with molester.

Fortunately, my students seemed blissfully unaware that they answered to a silly name. Eventually, we teachers even got over the shock, and a unique name ended up fitting a child perfectly by the end of the year.

I tried to conjure a grown-up version of Sneaker, Midgett and Purity, but all I could see was a prison cell, a sideshow and a floor-to-ceiling pole. As a child, I wanted to be named Stormy. It seemed mysterious and powerful, but hardly would have fit me.

I began to like my own name when, as an adult, I first read the *Little House on the Prairie* books. Prairie rhymes with Carrie, too, and I adore pioneer stories. Laura's little sister's name was Carrie. I craved their simple life and limited social obligations. The name Carrie brought to mind an old-fashioned girl, nervous and pale.

Suddenly, Carrie was the perfect name for me, and *Mrs. M.* was beginning to fit, too.

20
Inner Milk Bone Girl

Owen Charter passed a rule, banishing all games of tag on the playground. The "running tap" used to tag someone was often reported at home as, "That girl hit me!" which parents interpreted as bullying.

We teachers sadly informed our classes that tag, the cherished childhood game of all humans, was no longer allowed. That kind of authority seemed to come with the job, and I wondered what other irritants and time-wasters I could rid my classroom of. *Several* things, maybe.

I had similar veto power as a child, but I'd stumbled upon that by accident. When I was nine years old, my mother showed me a newspaper article about a girl my age, left alone in an abandoned apartment.

The girl figured out how to use the can opener and ate cold creamed corn, saving a box of stale Milk Bones for emergencies. She rinsed out her own T-shirts in the sink and walked to school on time. So it was a couple of weeks before anyone noticed something was wrong. In fact, the girl herself alerted a teacher that she was fresh out of dog biscuits and getting hungry.

I worried that my mother had shown me the article as a threat, and I began to prepare. I counted the cans of vegetables in the cabinet, checked the box of laundry soap, and I hoarded loose change in a clean jelly jar in my closet. It was painfully delicious to imagine being on my own.

Soon after that, my parents split up. My mother didn't abandon me but she did get a job, and I became one of the jillions of "latchkey kids" raising themselves in the '70s. My mother announced her new expectations: I was not to leave the house or answer the door. I was not to have friends over. I could make two phone calls per day, one to her at work and one to a friend for homework discussion only.

I was a good girl and didn't question her rules. Besides, my mother hadn't considered any other trouble I might dream up, and I was free to make further decisions for myself.

I did my homework immediately after school and then turned on the television. I sat a few inches from the screen in a lumpy bean bag chair, ruining my eyes because there was no one to tell me to scoot back. *Gilligan's Island* and *The Brady Bunch* became my immediate family.

I was an expert at heating vegetable oil in a pan until it smoked and then deep-frying tortilla chips or French fries. The freezer kept me entertained. I froze things, just to see what would happen: a balloon full of water, toothpaste, a flip flop. Latchkey kids had no smart electronic devices to babysit them. We survived on our own because we were bored and curious.

As a teacher, I missed the pure freedom and control that I'd enjoyed as a child. Some days, the frenzied workload had me raw on one side and burnt on the other. But if playground tag was no longer holy and could be banned from the school, then maybe I didn't have to tolerate other things either.

I decided to do a little old fashioned experimentation, latchkey kid style, just to see what would happen. Maybe I could mold my teaching career into more of a custom fit for me, and I could finally smooth out those nerves that still fuzzed up at times.

There were several things in class that interfered with student learning, wasted *my* time or were just plain gross. I flexed my teacher muscles and began to pare down the frustrating parts of the job.

I started with food, a constant problem in the classroom: peanut allergies and party treats, "nutrition" breaks and forgotten lunchboxes.

I thought back to the difficulty I'd had with food as a child. Around the same time I read about the Milk Bone girl, my birthday came and I asked for an angel food cake. My mother made one from a mix, with an airy whipped frosting.

I watched her slice colored marshmallows into pretty flowers for the top, helping myself to a few. Then I went on to bed thinking of sharing that beautiful cake with my friend, Gina, who was coming to play the next day.

Somehow, my cake was left overnight on the kitchen counter. When I looked at it the next morning, it was covered in a swarm of black ants. As a single parent, my mother did not waste food, and she could not afford a replacement cake mix. She picked as many ants as she saw out of the frosting and marshmallows, and then smoothed it back down with a spatula.

"Well, if there are any ants inside, they will just have to die. We can say they are chocolate sprinkles. No one will know."

I was sure they would know, but there was no arguing with her. That was my birthday cake, if I wanted one. It would be worse trying to explain not having any cake. Ashamed, I watched Gina and her sisters chew and swallow, imagining all those ants sliding down their throats, possibly still wiggling.

"Aren't you going to eat some cake?" Gina asked around a mouthful. Her ponytail bobbed as she chewed.

"I guess I'm not hungry."

I lied. I would have eaten those stale dog biscuits before the ant cake.

I never could stand extras in my food, and when I taught preschool, it got worse. Parents were responsible for providing the class with a snack from a list of healthy options. Most of them brought store-bought crackers in sealed boxes with plenty to go around, but I still had good reason to be leery.

We received cheese cubes cut at home on a dirty counter, with toast crumbs and jam smudges coating one side.

"Pigs in a blanket"—hot dogs baked in cheese, crescent dough, with black dog hair. The worst was a large Tupperware of trail mix. As I spooned it onto napkins, it stuck together with white threads. I showed it to the other teacher, Amy.

"Are those worms?" she asked, wrinkling her nose.

I nodded. "And they're spinning cocoons."

Amy had a stronger stomach than I did.

"Science table," she shrugged.

We couldn't serve children food like that. The child who brought and would recognize the snack was given a napkinful, while we threw the rest away. The preschool kept an emergency stash of little fish crackers and Fig Newtons for the other kids.

When I moved up from preschool to first grade, I hoped that the *Fear Factor* food challenges were behind me. By that time, many schools had stopped allowing students to bring in treats for birthdays or class parties.

These events took time away from the education process and could be a health issue with all the allergies and the question of home cleanliness. But Owen Charter wasn't picky. We allowed students to bring in anything: home-baked, store-bought or snacks with a hairy cheese filling.

What parents didn't realize was that, when a child brought in a treat, school stopped and teachers became waitresses. When "choices" became a popular child-rearing trend, I found myself offering each student a selection of treats.

"Tammy, would you like a chocolate or lemon cupcake? Pink or blue frosting? The Spiderman ring, or Barbie?" Sometimes, it was multiple types of cookies, or five flavors of Popsicles.

The classroom banquet went the way of tag. I sent home a letter, requesting that celebrations be limited to "one bite-sized cupcake per child, store-bought, lightly frosted in one flavor, and no jewelry."

Things that came *out* of kids' bodies could stop the education process, too. The few times I had to clean up first grader poop, I was grateful that I was no longer teaching toddlers.

One preschool day when I arrived for work, the other teacher, Amy, met me in the hallway. She did not great me with, "Good morning."

"I *would* do it," she said, "but I'm wearing a skirt."

I glanced at her clothing, and she was indeed wearing a floor-length gypsy skirt, in black and white paisley.

"Do what?" I started to ask, and then the smell hit me. I saw that the door to the preschool potty was closed. Amy opened the door a crack to show me.

"Dylan got sick. His mom already took him home."

The bathroom floor looked like a farm animal had been there. Piles and piles of loose poop shimmered like pudding on the floor. We had no school nurse or janitor at the preschool—just us teachers and the director.

If it weren't for the long skirt, Amy would have cleaned the floor. She was a lovely person and a hard worker. So we brainstormed the best approach to cleaning up, a stalling tactic on my part, and I finally went to the kitchen for a spoon.

Unfortunately, the largest spoon was slotted. I did the best I could with the bathroom floor and came out holding the gooey spoon at arms' length. A mother was standing there and put her hand up in the sign of 'stop.'

"I don't *even* want to know." She walked out.

I threw the spoon away and mopped up the rest with paper towels, then a bleach soaked mop, then disinfectant spray, and then a second coat of disinfectant spray. I loved Amy, but the next day, *I* wore a skirt.

Although I wanted to, there was no way to ban poop from the classroom. I tried scheduling official class bathroom breaks, giving extra turns, and allowing for emergencies, but tummy trouble happened. I could relate to those students. At least I knew how to comfort them, and it didn't make me nervous.

At Owen Charter, one thing I did take control of was Show and Tell. Teachers were required to present so much math and reading curriculum that there just wasn't time to get hijacked by stuffed unicorns, new hairbrushes and grubby plastic watches that didn't light up anymore.

Show and Tell was a virus, and once the class was infected, it was nearly impossible to recover. The only treatment was sternness and consequences for students, lengthy explanations to parents, and lots of sending home copies of policy from the school handbook.

The year tag was banned, my classroom was completely free of Show and Tell. No one brought anything and no one asked to bring anything. Then I had a substitute in my room for a couple of days. She invited the kids to bring Show and Tell. She *invited* them.

The first day, she'd caught Tessie putting a rock in her backpack. Even though rocks violated the school weapons rules, the substitute asked her to show the rock to the class. The next day, more students brought items from home. Little metal cars and balding dolls rather than rocks, but still this was against our "no toys at school" rules. Toys distracted from curriculum.

When I returned, more than half the class was bringing Show and Tell. To further the trouble, once I reinstated school rules, parents complained that their child didn't get a turn.

Administrators encouraged me to follow policy while keeping the parents happy and enrollment funding high. The message was clear: I had to make sure no one pulled their children out of our charter school over Show and Tell.

The initial outbreak eventually passed, but then the class came down with a secondary infection of Show and Tell, a plague. Students brought things that might apply to school curriculum: caterpillars in a jar, plants, rainbow DVDs. I even had a mother who wanted to do Show and Tell. She sent me a note, saying she'd be in to show the class how she makes homemade glue.

I took back my classroom with attitude. I was the teacher, had been for three years, and the students did not write my lesson plans. Neither did mothers with glue.

I thought of all the people I'd confronted over the Show and Tell issue. I'd been professional and assertive. I didn't always like the job, but I was becoming good at it. The classroom was almost my new best friend. But not quite.

Kids' trends seemed fun, but underneath their harmless appearance was a teacher's nightmare. Many of these trends had to be banned to keep attention focused on math and reading.

Shoes with wheels inside the sole, mechanical pets that talked, and noisy "slap" bracelets were confiscated for obvious reasons. Then came Silly Bandz—brightly colored rubbery bands in the shapes of animals, cars, and movie characters that sold for a couple of dollars for a few million of them.

One girl would arrive at school wearing an entire package on her right arm. By the time I took attendance that morning, most of the class had three or four Silly Bandz on their desks, admiring the shapes and stretchiness of non-round rubber bands. Because they were so cheap, they were very hard to get rid of. Even the most underprivileged students eventually had a whole bag of them.

The bands hung on ears, wrapped around pencils, or were used as handcuffs. Kids chewed a mouthful of them, shot them into the air and fought over them.

"I didn't *give* those to her. I was just letting her look at the pink ones!"

"If I can see or hear, or even *think* you have Silly Bandz, they are *mine!*"

My fast, decisive response made all the difference. And that worked until the press-on nail trend.

First graders who came to school in eye makeup or high heels were also a problem—but not as much as the press-on nails. Before long, instead of one girl wearing a set, ten girls were each wearing one nail.

They picked their noses with them, used them as bookmarks, chewed on them and poked other students with them. When I saw a child with press-on nails, I put all 10 nails in a zippy bag and sent them home on Friday.

Soon a new toy came to class: tiny, three-dimensional erasers in the shape and colors of a skunk, a doll or a cartoon character. Owen Charter foolishly featured them at our book fair and the school Santa Shop, giving them the appearance of being school-approved. After all, we *sold* them!

The problem was that children didn't use them as erasers. The eraser part was just an alibi. The girls put on little desk plays with them, while the boys used them to act out murders.

"Good morning, boys and girls," I'd say cheerfully. "Let's take out our crayon boxes for our morning paper."

Instead of quiet working sounds, I heard their comments.

"Hi horsey, will you be my friend?"

"Yes. Do you want to come to my desk for popcorn?"

Lukas stabbed his cat eraser with scissors

"Die! Die!"

"Boys and girls, we're *working* right now. Put the toys in your backpack and get started."

"These are erasers, Mrs. M." Bailee smiled sweetly. "My mom wants me to have them in case I make a mistake on my school work."

I looked into that, and the little things did indeed erase pencil marks. Still, they were a huge distraction and I wanted them gone. Any toy erasers that I saw or heard engaging in non-eraser activities were kept in my desk until a parent came to get them.

Mrs. Gardener allowed that stuff in her classroom. I admired her for it, as her class was more fun than mine. But that child-friendly method didn't work for me. It had been comforting when I was her student teacher and newly recovering from being fired, but three years later, it was too loose and chaotic for me.

I had developed my own teaching style, and I needed peace and order. The students in my class thrived on my comfort level: If Mrs. M. wasn't happy, no one was happy. Or more accurately, if my energy was being drained by silly stuff, I confiscated it.

It came to me then: there were many correct ways to teach. All kinds of kids needed all kinds of teachers. My own personality and struggles were part of what kept my learners interested.

I began to trust my professional judgment. *I* decided what influenced my students. I made executive decisions for their benefit. I rediscovered my inner Milk Bone girl, who liked being in charge, who had the authority to get rid of tag.

Still, I was sure there was a factory somewhere, staffed entirely with teachers gone bad, trashy teachers and teachers fired by Mrs. Hill. Their job was to create small toys that children could play with in class to avoid being educated.

When I stop teaching, I'll get a job there.

21
Livable Chunks

After three years, I began to recognize the teaching cycle—a menstrual cycle of sorts: I'd have worried if it didn't come at all, but I was glad when the whole mess was over for a while.

There was a cadence to the year at Owen Charter, and events occurred in a predictable order. I made a checklist for myself, a linear map of the year. Experience allowed me to see over and around obstacles, to remember the land mines and worry about them less. If something went wrong, I just checked it off as one step closer to summer.

Each year, I came to expect these events:

☑ *Bouts of Crying*

Starting mid-July, Mrs. Gardener called me every other day.

"Do we really have to go back to school?"

If even *she* felt depressed, then my crying was reasonable. I was hooked on the job, but not enough to leave the house. I'd force myself to go to crowded stores and stop hiding out, to listen to the TV and get used to noise.

☑ *Teachers Report for Duty*

Two weeks before the students would arrive, Principal Owen mailed a letter to all her staff. I punished the letter, ignoring it on the table for a couple of days.

Then the autumn thrill of a new school year, new kids and new clothes, lured me to tear into the envelope. Principal Owen wanted me *back*! My classroom was eager to be cleaned, unpacked and set up for students, who *needed* me.

☑ Meet the Teacher Night

The Friday before the first day of school, students, parents and grandmas with video cameras, rushed into my pristine classroom, which would never be pristine again.

Kids yelled, "I got Mrs. M!" or "I wanted Mrs. Gardener!"

I smiled either way. Walmart bags full of crayons, pencils and Kleenex piled up, and we teachers stayed late into the night, sorting and storing it all. I wondered what my life would be like when I opened the final box of this year's Kleenex.

☑ The Night Before the First Day of School

I lay awake most of the night, my heart pounding and my pillow squishy with sweat. I vowed to become a monk, who practiced infrequent eye contact and long periods of silence.

☑ Teacher Lore

Mrs. Gardener noted my bleary eyes before school on the first day.

"You know that losing sleep is a sign of a devoted teacher. Those eyes of yours are bragging rights!"

☑ First Day of School

The hardest part of every year for me was standing for the first time in front of all those new eyes, until kids who were strangers became kids who were mine. I rehearsed a starter speech.

"Good morning, and welcome to first grade."

The speech was my bridge from nerve overload to plain old jitters that I could manage.

> Note-to-self: Do *not* lose sleep next year!

☑ *4th Day Complaint*

At least one parent expressed concern that my assignments were too easy for her child.

"Maybe Amelia needs to be in the second grade," a mother would say.

I needed a few days, at least, to get the world of school spinning on its axis before the backseat teaching started.

☑ *The Other 4th Day Complaint*

At least one different parent complained that my assignments were too hard.

"We can't figure out these math sheets where you do addition and color a picture of something."

The year suddenly felt long.

☑ *Request to Change Rooms*

During the first week of school, a concerned mother would urgently inform me that her daughter was afraid of me and must change rooms immediately. She was sure her child would like the other first grade teacher, Mrs. Gardener, much better. I was sure she would too, but I stopped being hurt by this. It was always followed by the:

☑ *Request to Stay*

"Mrs. M., I'm so glad you recommended giving it time. Emily *loves* you. She's very happy in your class."

I told myself to just check it off. Summer was on the way.

☑ *Large Chunk of Missing Hair*

Not mine. Toward the end of August, at least one of my students tried out her new little plastic scissors by cutting her own hair down to the scalp and dropping it on the floor for me to identify. I spent lunch puzzling over who, of 30 kids, had the long brown hair this year. Then I placed the hair in a zippy bag, called parents, confiscated scissors and recommended hair salons that specialized in children. The self-scalping was always done by a child participating that same evening in the:

☑ *Owen Charter Talent Show*

Between the original poetry, un-choreographed flailing dances and made-up songs, another child would stand solemnly at the microphone and preach a sermon. The audience was invited to spend eternity in hell, unless we left our sinful ways behind. I'd clap anyway. It was a fun twist to watch the audience squirm instead of me.

☑ *Teacher Lore*

Owen Charter teachers kept regular paper grade books, rather than online records. We waited about three weeks to write the students' names in ink in alphabetical order. The minute we finished, at least two kids would drop out and flaw the grade book. I used this to my advantage in larger classes and wrote the names early. The trick never failed to relieve me of excess enrollment.

☑ *First Quarter Report Cards*

As a child, I eagerly waited to see what my teacher said about me. I was a "good girl," an "excellent student," and advised to "speak up." I kept this in mind when writing my own report cards. In the first quarter, they were simple and welcoming.

"I enjoy having your child in class."

And it was true that early in the year.

☑ *Fall Break*

I could hardly bear to check it off. I needed the week to catch my emotional breath and get multiple loads of laundry dry at home. Two weeks would have been better.

☑ *Parent-Teacher Conferences*

Every year a parent informed me, "You seem like a nice teacher—not at all the monster my child says you are."

Monster? My mother would never have said that to one of my childhood teachers. How had I possibly come across as a monster? This baffled me. Maybe I was a gentle monster, big and scary, but kind-hearted.

☑ *Teacher Lore*

Teachers liked to say that if we made it past Halloween, we could make it to the end of the year. The kids were trained, the kinks worked out and real teaching and learning took over. It was soothing to feel the pleasant rush of days.

☑ *The Day after Halloween*

At least two children vomited candy in the classroom.

☑ *New Kids*

It was common in late fall for parents to get new jobs and students to move away. The children who replaced them often came from waitlists, or they had been kicked out of other schools for behavior. It only took one personality to throw off classroom dynamics. I tried not to torture myself with memories of the Screamers that had ruined my classes before. We accepted the new personalities into our group.

☑ *Holiday Factory*

Around Thanksgiving, parents complained that Owen Charter had too many parties, or not enough parties. I understood; those dreadful parties were what I remembered from school too. Still, my job was to teach reading and math.

☑ *Winter Holidays Musical Performance*

We offended all religious preferences with our programs: Too much baby Jesus, not enough baby Jesus and the odd Japanese song that sounded like curse words. I enjoyed the break in routine—the way the songs stuck in my head at night when I got up to use the bathroom. I was as scared and proud to be on stage as my students were.

☑ Winter Break

At home, I kept a special box of Christmas ornaments, given to me by students. I didn't want the constant school reminder on my tree at home, but I had to keep them. I was a teacher.

☑ Teacher Lore

Mrs. Gardener and I reminded each other that students always matured over winter break. We were pleasantly surprised by their maturity and self-control when school resumed.

☑ Tour the School

Starting January 2nd, over-achieving parents brought tantrumming four-year-olds to visit Owen Charter and enroll them in the next year's kindergarten. At least one parent would admit something like, "My older son has been taking care of Stephen since I went back to work. He's a big fan of *Lord of the Rings* and only speaks Elvish to Stephen. Do any of the teachers here speak Elvish?"

I considered finding a new job before Stephen moved on to first grade.

☑ Second Quarter Report Cards

These were tricky. Teachers were required to discuss retention with parents of lower-achievers. I became proficient at phrases like, "would benefit from another year," or "develop skills he needs to become successful," or "the gift of time..." No child would be left behind—except theirs.

☑ *100ᵗʰ Day of School*

We didn't celebrate this when I was a child. Now, my lesson plans included activities such as jumping 100 times and displaying bags of 100 raisins or barrettes. It was the day schools received state funding for the year, and it no longer mattered if parents pulled their kids out of school. Mrs. Gardener called it *The Day I Stop Being Nice.*

☑ *Science Fair*

The more competitive first graders presented projects about DNA or lightning. My personal favorites were the projects thrown together that morning by a frantic mother. Two cups and a string with a note that read, "Put this in the science fair. We'll be in later with the video camera."

I could well imagine a child's crying fit that must have precipitated those entries.

☑ *Valentine's Day*

I received some lovely gifts, like roses and candy, but I preferred kids' crayon-written notes declaring that I was the best teacher ever in the whole wide world. They were absolutely right! I was tempted to copy and mail the notes to Mrs. Hill as proof of my success.

☑ *Third Quarter Report Cards*

By March, it was all I could do to keep from commenting, "I'm *so* glad your child does not live in my home."

Occasionally, I received a surprise, when a non-reader began to read fluently.

"I wish I had a whole classroom of Emmas!" was the highest praise.

☑*Spring Break*

I couldn't wait to check it off: the next stop was summer. First, I had to get through the spring vomiting illnesses and the bickering kids that no seating arrangements could cure.

☑*Standardized Tests*

How could I avoid teaching to the test or at least practicing similar test questions? Part of my salary depended on scores. The test took nearly a week. I comforted crying students, fed granola bars to breakfast skippers and erased drawings from bubble-in answer sheets. Some kids stayed home and avoided the whole test. My own second grade teacher had given us each one marshmallow for finishing. That probably wouldn't have worked with the kids of today.

☑*Contracts*

I gossiped with the other teachers. *Who would get the bigger room? Who accepted a job at a rival public school?* The end of the year was not a good time to offer me a new contract. By that time, I was not enamored with teaching anymore, and was as likely to spill my soda on it as sign it.

☑ *Next Year's Supply List*

I was out of wipies and Kleenex. I had a handful of pink erasers left. What I really wanted from parents was a box of respect, a soft-pack of patience, some help in assorted colors.

☑ *Classroom Inventory*

Every item in my classroom, from markers to chairs, had to be counted, because first graders loved to steal old textbooks and plain office staplers—something to remember first grade by.

☑ *Fourth Quarter Report Cards*

"Keep reading and have a great summer!" I'd write joyously on each one.

I was sure that my teachers back in the '70s felt exactly the same.

☑ *Teacher Lore*

Mrs. Gardener and I assured each other that good classes alternated. One year, I'd have an exhausting group of street-wise potty mouths, and the next—a sweet bunch of huggers. I earned them.

☑ *The Last Day of School*

I couldn't wait to miss all those kids, but first I had to present awards at the assembly. When I was a child, my teacher gave me a certificate for my quietness and an ability to write.

I wondered if my students would remember their awards. I dressed in a pretty skirt and rehearsed a speech about the terrific year and smart students.

As soon as I lined my class up on stage, I looked directly into the eyes of 500 parents to get past the nausea. I spoke slowly, making myself miserable but present, and announced the achievements of each student in my care: book reports, math facts, a good friend.

When it was over, several teachers would ask me what my secret was.

"We love to hear you speak at assemblies."

How could I explain what it took for me to stand in front of people? That I'd been known to pass out, that I'd been fired from student teaching, that even my skin hurt some days, or that I loved teaching kids to read more than anything, and that's what made it all worth it.

With the school year mapped out into livable chunks, I thought I owned the job. Teaching was mine, even if the next year would start with:

☑ *Bouts of Crying*

22
Puff

Owen Charter Christmas musicals were fancy productions. Teachers' lesson plans included daily stage rehearsals. Music class became lyric memorization, while art time was used for painting sets. At lunch, I stopped by Mrs. Gardener's classroom to remind her of the afternoon rehearsal.

I paused at her doorway and tried to make sense of what I saw. Her red hair was growing in gray. Her desk was buried under a scuffle of papers. Kid debris covered the floor.

"Are you okay?" I asked.

"Yeah. Just aggravated. Yesterday I gave a spelling test, graded the papers and sent them home for practice. This kid in my class, Devin, scored only eight words out of 30. His mom came to see me just now and told me she didn't appreciate me correcting him. She said, 'Devin has my permission to spell words any way he wants.'"

"What? She can't give permission to misspell words."

This sounded like a good story, so I pulled up a kid's plastic chair.

"Apparently 'permission' means that a mother can force the rest of the world to bend to her wishes. I told her to have him write each misspelled word three times and he'd do better on the next test, but she said she only wants smiley face stickers on his papers from now on."

I nodded in understanding of Mrs. Gardener's frustration.

"I once turned down a job at a preschool," I told her. "The director said her students had permission to do whatever they wanted and that my job would be to make any of it possible. She told me several of the children enjoyed returning to school in the evenings and walking in paint after the teachers had cleaned."

"Oh, I bet they did," said Mrs. Gardener.

"She also told me that if a child wanted to play in the street, then it was up to me stop traffic."

"What was the job description? *Puff, the Magic Dragon?*" she asked.

"Puff, the Magic Teacher, I guess." The lyrics stuck in my head the rest of the day. *One gray night it happened. Jackie Paper came no more. And Puff that mighty dragon, he ceased his fearless roar. Without his lifelong friend, Puff could not be brave. So Puff, that mighty dragon, sadly slipped into his cave.*

That afternoon, Principal Owen clarified to the mother that teachers were mandated to correct students' work and that Mrs. Gardener was doing a fine job. The situation was resolved, but she was still stewing. The next day, my teaching buddy was absent.

During rehearsal, our music director announced that two new parts had been added to the program: dancing teeth for the song, *All I Want for Christmas.* The teeth would not be speaking or singing, but the kids would wear white costumes and dance across the stage.

Our music director tapped a pencil on her clipboard.

"Mrs. M., do you have any kids you could assign to these special parts as a reward? Maybe someone from your class and someone from Gardener's class, who has never had consequences?"

Then it came to me, like a Christmas angel.

"Mrs. Gardener will do it."

A spot in the play was just what she needed.

The director shook her head.

"She's not here today."

"I know, but she can start tomorrow."

"I like your idea—giving a popular teacher a cameo spot, but I need *two* teeth."

I heard myself say, "I'll do it. I'll do it, too!"

I'd be hidden deep inside a costume right next to Mrs. Gardener. I wasn't as popular as she was, but the early childhood teachers were always recognizable at Owen Charter.

I called her at home that night as I was changing into around-the-house comfies.

"I have a surprise for you," I said. "You and I are going to be dancing teeth in the Christmas musical."

"Dancing what?"

"*Teeth.*"

"Oh, that will teach me to take a day off," she complained.

"Come on! I'm cheering you up."

"Okay, sure. We'll be teeth together. It could be fun."

"You just gave yourself permission to be happy. See? Permission can be given for anything. I, myself, have permission *not* to be nervous anymore. I just haven't taken myself up on it, yet."

"Okay, then I have permission to block Wednesdays from memory, or at least those awful spelling tests."

"That's the way! See you in the morning."

"I love you, Mrs. M. Thanks for caring."

The tooth costumes were white pillow cases, painted with smiling girl faces and ponytails made of yarn. Hers was yellow, and mine was red. They didn't fit either of us. I took them home, added fabric, and cut eye holes.

We had to hold our hands up to the corners to keep them tooth-shaped and not head-shaped. It was an awkward and uncomfortable position to stay in, and we practiced swaying side to side and lifting our feet across the stage.

Grades kindergarten through third rehearsed the Christmas musical daily for three weeks. We ran our students up and down the stairs from the stage to the basement for costume changes, new props, bathroom emergencies and the last minute yellow duck costume that Principal Owen insisted would liven up the show.

Mrs. Gardener didn't like keeping track of our lyrics and stage placements, so I did the organization for both classes.

And then it came time for us teeth.

Our first grade classes stood on risers dress-rehearsing, and Mrs. Gardener and I waited behind the black curtain for our cue to dance. The poorly-placed eye holes I'd cut made it difficult to see. My spunky aide that year, Sasha, waited on the other side and her job was to quietly call, "This way… this way."

The piano played and the kids sang, *All I Want for Christmas…* Mrs. Gardener and I danced onto the stage. All was going well. I could hear Sasha whispering, "This way," and I moved towards her voice.

Then I heard, "Mrs. Gardener, this way. Mrs. Gardener? *Mrs. Gardener!*"

Then a scream and a crash.

The piano stopped. I peeked out of one eyehole and saw Mrs. Gardener topple off the stage.

"I'm not hurt," she called out. "I just can't see where I'm going." She lay tangled in her pillow case and yellow yarn ponytail. I felt so horrible looking down at her crumpled self. I'd made her be a tooth, I'd cut the eyes in the costumes. She was *Mrs. Gardener*. How could I have let her fall?

I suddenly realized that the relationship was changing for my teaching buddy and me. I didn't depend on her for guidance anymore. She'd long since given me the first grade curriculum to keep in my files—all the worksheets, the reading books and the supplies. She was my friend now, my sister in teaching, and no longer my security blanket. And this year, she needed me to remind *her*, to cheer her up, to help her organize, to watch out for her.

In time for our performance that evening, Sasha and I placed bright green masking tape across the stage to guide us teeth, to guide Mrs. Gardener, as we danced.

The audience was full of mothers, fathers, toddlers, siblings, grandparents and out-of-town company. It also included my own mother, husband and our boy. I was tempted to peek conspicuously around the black curtain and wave at everyone, just to confront the butterflies in my stomach.

While I listened for our musical cue, time stopped. In that instant, there was just me and all of this wonderful school life. I was a *teacher*—something I had wanted since I was four years old. I had a beautiful classroom, 30 fairly well-behaved kids that year, a teacher friend I adored. I practically had an apple on my desk.

All those thoughts drifted through the air and landed on me, like glitter on the stage. If I had nothing else, I would always have that one moment—the best of times. Maybe the half-way mark in my life.

I looked at all I'd been given in exchange for the sting of being fired from student teaching. The night's flash of success mostly made up for the difficulties in getting there.

And then we danced.

The audience clapped and cheered until we hid again behind the black curtain, pulling the pillow case tooth costumes off of our clothes.

Mrs. Gardener held up her costume by its yellow ponytail.

"This was fun! I'm glad you volunteered us," she said, out of breath.

My heart pounded and my eyes adjusted to the darkness backstage.

"I wish we could keep our costumes to remember it by. Just think—I was a *tooth* in a school play!"

"We'll remember," she laughed. "Who could forget? My ankle still hurts."

She paused to fix her hairclip and took one deep breath.

"I'm going to retire in May."

I knew. I'd sensed it all year. She'd been with me every day that I'd worked at Owen Charter. Hundreds of days—and every one had been made better, more manageable—because she was in the classroom next to mine. I'd had disappointments in teaching before, but this one would hurt. It was a loss so hard that I could feel it chasing me down. I held still and let it catch me.

She went on.

"I'll miss you—don't doubt that for a second. But it's time. My life *needs* me."

I dropped the tooth costume, just an old pillowcase and some red yarn. It was never mine to keep anyway.

I hugged her, and we herded our students down to the basement for one final costume change and a wish of Merry Christmas to the audience. The beautiful program was over.

It took an hour to send students home with the right parents, and we didn't meet up again. Mrs. Gardener called me during Christmas break.

"Think about this," she said. "The school will hire someone to replace me next year, and you get the fun of teaching her everything you know. That's all I did when you came to me as a student teacher."

"You got me because I'd been fired."

"Fired-shmired. You're Mrs. M!"

"*Mrs. M.* is not the kind of character that teachers here are supposed to be," I told her. "I don't sing and dance in class like you do. I don't wear clown wigs, like Mrs. Owen, and I never could make myself talk to a hairy puppet."

"You're Puff! Puff the Magic Dragon, remember? Kids *love* you!"

I tried to smile, but the confident Mrs. M. was suddenly an illusion. Without Mrs. Gardener, I couldn't be brave. My Jackie Paper was retiring, and she wouldn't be coming back. The time to frolic with a teaching buddy was over, and so was my fearless roar. I sadly slipped into my cave, and the darkness stayed beyond the holidays.

In a way, my childhood desire to teach was satisfied. I'd proven to myself that I could be a teacher, and I was successful for nearly three years now. Without Mrs. Gardener to make it fun, and now to take care of, I was ready to be done with kids' behavior, entitled parents and mopping bathrooms. Without Mrs. Gardener, these events would not be entertainment. The job would be heavy and time-consuming.

I considered that it might be right for me to lay teaching down, if that's how I felt about it—to rest my anxious muscles. I'd already tried casework, and that hadn't been a good fit. I could work at the library, shelving comfortable old books, or at Kmart, stocking pretty shampoo bottles that couldn't argue with me, or an office, where I wasn't on my feet all day—anywhere that wouldn't remind me that I'd once known Mrs. Gardener.

I filled out a couple of applications, but didn't turn them in. Finally, I compromised and interviewed at a private school; still teaching, but in fresh surroundings. I didn't get the job.

Eventually, our massive spring workload took over. There were things, I reasoned, to like about teaching at Owen Charter: a big sticky art project, the yearly musical, some of the families and reading—always reading. I had figured out a lot about the job on my own. Profiling, that was all me! And baking cookies with 30 kids was something even Mrs. Gardener wouldn't try.

Owen Charter had never been my first choice; I went there to spite Mrs. Hill. But I began to think that maybe I would try it *without* Mrs. Gardener—just to see.

I thought back to my first day with her, when she held my shaky hands in hers. *No matter what, you will be a teacher.*

I thought of locking eyes with a child's as he realized he could read. I thought of my mother, who bought me an antique slate and set of *McGuffey Readers*, like Laura Ingalls had used, because I was a teacher.

I enjoyed the sheltering, self-contained world of Owen Charter, and I didn't want to have to start over again. I even ate candy I found on the playground, and if that didn't say Owen Charter, then nothing did.

Principal Owen offered me lead teacher pay and accepted my signed contract with, "Yeah! My first grade program remains intact!" I appreciated her confidence, but I'd sold another year of my life.

Finally, at an end of the year staff meeting, as I sat sweating and hand-wringing, never comfortable in a large group, I suddenly noticed how calm everyone else seemed, despite the crowded seating. I imagined the thoughts of each person there.

Someone was writing her grocery list, others were texting, one woman was cleaning out her purse while another blew her nose. They probably weren't feeling like rotten teachers, and they certainly weren't finding fault with me.

I'd already had to give up Mrs. Gardener; she wasn't even at the staff meeting. Maybe I was just letting anxious thoughts run away with me. Maybe I'd always put too much thought into every action, my own and those of other people.

As a test, I let the anxiety stop for a minute. Could I be as comfortable as everyone else seemed to be? The earth didn't shake. I didn't fall apart into little piles of skin, tears and nerves. I was fine just breathing and being in the middle of all these people.

And I realized my own thoughts had contributed to my nervous misery all these years. Since childhood, I'd been telling myself that I wasn't competent, wasn't good enough and couldn't be successful.

I had already given myself permission. I imagined laying my anxiety down on the floor in a little furry pile, like a pet monster. Poor frightened thing!

I made a new promise. I'd care for it and provide for its needs, step over it and make arrangements for it if I went away. I'd feed it and play with it; keep it on a leash and make sure it didn't run out the door. But sometimes I would forget about it, and that would have to be okay.

I was a busy and competent anxiety-owner now, and a teacher, with other concerns.

On the last day of school, I stood in the doorway between Mrs. Gardener's classroom and mine. Her car was already packed full of books and other personal items that she wanted to keep from her lifetime of teaching. I watched, silent and lonely, as she turned in a slow circle for one last look around her kid-stinky and still-cluttered classroom.

She turned suddenly and flung her arms around me.

"I have never loved working with anyone more than you. Just think—I worked with *Mrs. M.*"

I smiled.

"Take care of yourself then," I said. "You know… when I'm not around to look after you."

Maybe Puff could call Jackie sometimes, and they'd meet for lunch.

After Mrs. Gardener left, I went into the tiny kids' bathroom and wiped my eyes with toilet paper. The last box of Kleenex had long since been used by children. I looked around the bathroom: the sink, where countless globs of finger paint had been washed away; the floor, where sick kids got rid of their breakfast; and the door that I had I leaned against for moments of peace.

It was the same bathroom that naked screaming Monica had run from, three years earlier.

I looked into the mirror and said, "*You* are a teacher!"

23
Where Are They Now?

I often run into the people I wrote about at Owen Charter.

Mrs. Hill, who fired me from student teaching, has since purged her classroom of two more student teachers. I take comfort in knowing that it wasn't *all* my fault.

Her outcasts and I have taken steps to make sure she is not in charge of student teachers anymore. While I don't want to be at her mercy again, I certainly learned a lot about the classroom from her. Because of her, I assert myself, well before trouble starts.

As it turns out, she was wrong, though. There *is* a place for me in the teaching profession. Mrs. Hill shops at the same grocery store that I do. I don't hate her now, and that feels good. To use the words of Dr. Seuss, "We both smile, and we say 'hi.'"

Screamer Monica, attends a nearby elementary school. Her cousin tells me that Monica is still "wild and crazy." I imagine naked scissor-throwing would be hard to give up. Monica seared something like fear into my brain, and every year I beg, *Please, don't let me get another child like her in my class!* Then I remind myself that, because of Monica, I am an experienced teacher.

Tyson, who injured staff members and kids alike, was withdrawn from Owen Charter, and I didn't see him again. A friend of a friend works with his mother. Word has it that he is still a strong, hefty boy, but he is "getting help" in public school.

On thrift store sale days, I see Mr. Linnert, who wore the tin foil hats and sat in his lawn chair in the back of my classroom. He always speaks to me and asks about teaching. He is no longer wearing the hats, at least not when I see him.

My mother has had a few more health scares since the bone cancer miracle, but she is happy and still living.

Mrs. Gardener is, to this day, one of my dearest friends. She calls often to ask about that "book of crazy school stories" and to tell me I need to have more fun. She's soul candy.

There is a teaching gene. I have it, and I recognize one child in every class who has it. Usually, it's a girl who's organized, attentive, helpful, likes to watch me grade and wants to be in front of the class. It would be wrong for me to tell her the job isn't what she thinks, that she's wearing chalkboard-colored glasses.

I wish teaching hadn't changed so much since the '70s when I was a child, sitting in a circle of stuffed animals and drawing with chalk. *That* job would have been a good fit for me! In the years since I started teaching, disruptive students and adversarial parents have become commonplace.

Paperwork and after-school responsibilities are often overwhelming. State standards are giving way to the highly debated Common Core standards and keep the job in constant upheaval. It's not the job a lot of teachers dream of, or train for. The profession has one of the highest burn-out rates.

When I have a year that makes me want to leave, I file away the whole experience in the "hideous" box in my head. I rid the classroom of all its contaminated decorations and buy fresh. I tell myself the next year has to be better.

Some years *are* better, and they take me back to that first precious teaching time in Mrs. Gardener's classroom, with its safe smells of sweaty sneakers and cherry Chapstick.

Like a vampire, teaching sunk its magical teeth into me. My turning point was profiling the types of kids I'd always have in class, which allowed me to get control of the job and make it a better fit for me. The people at Owen Charter never criticized or punished me for being nervous. Not once. That made me comfortable enough to find my own way.

At a recent Meet the Teacher night, a former student introduced his little brother to me.

"Your teacher is Mrs. M.," he said. "Do you want to know how to make Mrs. M. happy?"

I thought, *Yes I do. Tell me how to be happy.*

My former student looked at his brother in all seriousness and said, "Learn to read and *like* it."

And yes, that would make me happy.

There are a few things I owe to teaching. The constant practice in front of people calloused my nerves better than any anxiety medication; I know now that nerves don't mean panic, as nerves mean *move*. I am more patient with kids, and I can pick my battles.

I am articulate in the professional world, willing to confront. I am not a natural leader, but I have learned how to lead, and the kids follow me. I can also chase a natural leader away when they try to take over for me. Best of all, I can teach another human being to read, no matter how my own insides tangle.

While I have earned every ounce of confidence, I am hardwired towards nervousness. The job is a constant pull against my own nature, but I show up every day and try hard. I do it for those certain students I was meant to know, and for the savory bits of success that make teaching worth the trouble. And a lot of days, *it is.*

I don't see myself putting in a lifetime of teaching, the way Mrs. Gardener did. But who knows? I keep going back every year. Eventually, for whatever reason, my time in the classroom will come to an end. At least I can say I won the struggle of nerves for a while and that, once upon time, I was a teacher.

~Mrs. M.

Acknowledgements

A special thank you to my husband for scraping me off the ceiling on more than one occasion. Thank you to my mother who doesn't like memoir as a genre, but read mine in one night.

There would be no teaching story without Principal Owen, who gave me a safe place to learn how. I deeply appreciate all the wonderful aides I have worked with at Owen Charter over the years: W.T., C.Y., and B.D.— you made it doable and so much more fun. And to spunky Sasha, for believing I should. A special "love you" to Mrs. Gardener's aide, Mrs. O'Rourke, who stood quietly beside me on the playground before she ever knew we'd be friends.

Thank you Mrs. K., Mrs. H., and Mrs. S. who allowed me to interview them about teaching practices in the '70s. They confirmed my belief that the job was a lot more fun back then. A big thanks to Mrs. H., who also let me get my feet on the ground.

A pleasant hello to the ladies in the Writers' Workshop: Vicky Young, Leota Hoover, Elaine Jordan, Carole Bolinski, Gretchen Phelps, and Colette Ward, who read anything I gave them and tried so hard not to hurt my feelings. To my first readers: Saralou Satton, who gave me courage, and to Toni Denis, Stephanie Jefferson, and John Rust who laughed the whole way through the first draft even though it wasn't supposed to be funny. To Marian Powell who said, "You've gotta write this stuff down."

And loads of love to Mrs. Gardener for making sure I got my tea set. Some girls never do get tea sets.

Carrie Malinowski was a successful teacher and reading tutor for many years. She now enjoys working with anxiety sufferers in behavioral health. She has a degree in psychology and an Arizona teaching certificate.

Carrie is the author of the children's book, *Hand-Me-Down Bear* (Heart to Heart Publishing, 2012), and a contributor to the *Chicken Soup for the Soul* series, including *Food and Love and Kids on the Spectrum*.

She lives in Arizona with her husband, son, and her dog, Chester.

Visit her at www.carriemalinowski.com.